JAMAICA

A Guide to the People, Politics and Culture

Marcel Bayer

IRP

The Latin America Bureau is an independent research and publishing organisation. It works to broaden public understanding of issues of human rights and social and economic justice in Latin America and the Caribbean.

First published in the UK in 1993 by Latin America Bureau (Research and Action) Ltd, 1 Amwell Street, London EC1R 1UL

Published in Jamaica and the Caribbean by Ian Randle Publishers, 206 Old Hope Road, Kingston 6, Jamaica

Dutch language edition published by Royal Tropical Institute, 63 Mauritskade, 1092 AD Amsterdam, and Novib, The Hague, the Netherlands

A CIP catalogue record for this book is available from the British library

ISBN 0 906156 81 5 (LAB)
ISBN 976 8100 19 2 (IRP)

Translated by: John Smith
Edited by: James Ferguson
Cover photograph by: Harry Gruyaert/Magnum
Cover design by: Andy Dark
Design by: Vincent Peters
Cartography by: Kees Prins and Marius Rieff Jr
Printed by: SSN - Nijmegen, the Netherlands

Trade distribution in the UK by: Central Books, 99 Wallis Road, London E9 5LN
Distribution in North America by: Monthly Review Press, 122 West 27th Street, New York, NY 10001

CONTENTS

Schoolchildren in uniform hurrying
home during a tropical downpour.
(Michael Kooren)

INTRODUCTION

In songs, films and books Jamaica has been romanticised as the *Island in the Sun*. Its exotic reputation rests on its paradise beaches, its lush green interior, the spectacular Blue Mountains and, naturally, its multi-ethnic people, descendants of Africans, Europeans and Asians.

The mix of American and African culture, in particular, has proved a fertile source of creativity in music, theatre and religion. Jamaica is the cradle of reggae, with its origins in the island's earlier styles of mento and ska and with strong influences from jazz, rhythm and blues and later rock'n'roll.

But reggae is more than just a musical trend. It is an outlet for the youth of the ghetto and expresses the search for a personal identity amidst poverty and deprivation. In this respect, reggae is closely associated with the Rastafarians and their quest for roots, historical and cultural. The 'Return to Africa' movement and the use of 'ganja' (marijuana) are two of the best-known expressions of this religious and cultural phenomenon.

At the same time, Jamaica is a fragmented society. The rich and a considerable section of the middle class have done well from the relatively liberal policies pursued since independence in 1962. Even the period of 'democratic socialism' in the 1970s made few inroads into their wealth. The prosperity of the new part of Kingston, the capital, and along the tourist north coast is conspicuous. People live there in total isolation in a world of their own, with little concept of, let alone contact with their fellow Jamaicans on the other side of the fence.

A ride through the poor downtown ghettoes of Kingston presents a completely different picture. Here people live with practically nothing and little expectation of a better life. In other large towns and in the rural interior the situation is not much better. Deprivation and poverty are everywhere, confronting Jamaica with its greatest, and potentially most explosive, problems today. And this despite the island's fertile soil and rich mineral resources.

This explains perhaps why there is so much aggression and violence in Jamaica, for this is the other, less romantic, face of Jamaica, the *Island in the Sun*.

| HISTORY

The Jamaicans: 'out of many one people'

Unity in diversity; 'out of many one people' is the national motto of Jamaica. The population of this Caribbean island has mixed origins. There are the descendants of Africans, Lebanese, Chinese, Indians and Arabs to be found alongside emigrants from a number of European countries. This great diversity of background and traditions provides for a fascinating mosaic of cultural expression.

The national motto with its ideal of unity, however, bears little relation to reality since there are sharp divisions within Jamaican society, based as often as not on skin colour. The motto, not without good reason, is based more on a hope, for Jamaican history is characterised by resistance and struggle, by the search for common roots and for a way out of poverty and dependence. Jamaicans are rightly proud of their past and, in particular, of the contribution made to it by the majority black population. But this history has not been without its conflict, violence and tragedy.

■ Nature, Arawaks and Spaniards

There are always ash-grey clouds hanging above the Blue Mountains. This mountain chain in the island's east, with summits some 2,500 metres high, is home to the island's most spectacular natural beauty. Clear mountain streams with falls and rapids, and a fantastic variety of tropical plant life provide the backdrop for the legends of the African slaves, the Maroons, who fled the plantations and heroically resisted oppression. Within this impenetrable region live the descendants of the slaves, as did their ancestors, in small and isolated settlements.

In another highly inaccessible region, Cockpit Country on the island's west side, there are also living descendants of the Maroons. The undulating emerald-green hill country, typical of Jamaica's interior, here turns into a fantastic limestone massif with mysterious caves and bizarrely shaped outcrops. For the rebelling slaves it was an ideal place to settle, since they could not be reached by the English troops. Places such as Maroon Town and Accompong are still the symbol for Jamaicans of the struggle against slavery and the craving for freedom.

The landscape of the Blue Mountains and Cockpit Country indicates both Jamaica's volcanic and oceanic origins. Many hundreds of millions of years ago, phenomenal forces brought about folds in the earth's crust, forming a garland of islands in today's Caribbean region. On the flanks of the volcanoes and the mountain ridges, the elements weathered away what had once been the ocean floor. The massif produced vegetation and was cut through by rivers. The interaction of the sea and erosion brought limestone plateaus into existence, where precipitation formed caves and rivers. It is in this limestone region that the island's most important export product, bauxite, is extracted. Over a large area the red clay covers the limestone in a thick layer, in some places several metres thick. Huge draglines scour the landscape and scrape away the 'red gold'.

Around the island, coastal plains of sand, gravel and clay were formed. Because of the ocean currents, the coastal strip on the north side is narrower than that on the south side of the island. The north side is Jamaica's main tourist area; the south coast is used more for agricultural production.

Indians Of the very first inhabitants of the island, the Arawaks, there remains little but traces of their civilisation. The Arawaks, an Indian people from the coastal region of what today is Venezuela and Guyana, settled in Jamaica in about 700 BC. From traces found of settlements and utensils, it is clear that they inhabited the whole island.

On 4 May 1492 Christopher Columbus landed at Dry Harbour, now called Discovery Bay, on Jamaica's north coast. He called the island Santiago. Columbus spoke of *'the fairest island that eyes have beheld; mountainous and the land seems to touch the sky...full of valleys and fields.'*

After some initial hostilities, he succeeded in gaining the confidence of the Indian *caciques* or chiefs. The inhabitants made a great impression on him. He referred to them as *'honest and content with what they have...a peaceful and generous people.'*

This was not surprising. Thinking that the Spaniards were immortal gods, the Arawaks regaled the newcomers with splendid feasts and presented them with their most beautiful ornaments. At first, the Spanish interest in gold aroused no suspicion among the Arawaks.

The Arawaks were a peaceful people. They lived on fish, the fruits of the trees and on a modest scale they cultivated cassava, maize and sweet potatoes. A favourite pastime was smoking tobacco. In fact the Spaniards took the word *tabaco* from the Arawaks, although this was their word for the pipe in which they used to smoke the leaves.

Another legacy of the indigenous population was the hammock, made of cotton and dyed in bright colours. Jamaica was to remain famous for its cotton fabrics well into the Spanish colonial period. The Spaniards had sailcloth made there for their ships.

In the summer of 1504, during his fourth voyage to the New World, Columbus was forced to return to the north coast of Jamaica after his ship had suffered heavy damage. For a whole year, he had to remain with his crew in the bay of Santa Gloria, now St Ann's Bay.

Spanish planters   The first colonisation dates from 1510. A group of Spaniards, under the leadership of Governor Juan de Esquivel, founded the settlement of Sevilla la Nueva near St Ann's Bay. It was about this time that the old name which the Arawaks had given their island, Xaymaca, first began to appear in books.

The Spanish colonisation was not altogether successful. Hardly any precious metal was found. According to contemporary chronicles, within a few years of the settlement by the colonists practically all the island's gold was in Spanish hands. This consisted primarily of the golden ornaments which the Arawaks had obtained by trading with neighbouring islands.

Nor did the foundation of a new capital, Villa de la Vega (now called Spanish Town) on the south side of the island, improve the colony's fortunes. Jamaica was used by passing ships as a base for refitting and taking on provisions. Other than that, the island was of little importance to Spain, even though the colonists did introduce new plants and fruit, such as sugar-cane, bananas and citrus fruits, to the island.

The most drastic change, of course, was the eradication of the original inhabitants. The Spaniards brought with them diseases such as smallpox, measles and bubonic plague. These took a heavy toll among the Indians, while many Arawaks also lost their lives as the result of severe corporal punishment and massacres by the Spanish colonists who forced them to work as serfs. In 1598, the then Governor of Jamaica, Fernando Melgarejo, drew attention to the alarmingly rapid decrease of the Indian population. In order to prevent the Arawaks from becoming extinct, he proposed to designate a special area where they could live in accordance with their own traditions and customs. The plantation owners saw no advantage in this plan, and as a result in 1655, when the English took power, there were no longer any Arawaks left in Jamaica.

To replace the Indian serfs the colonists bought African slaves. But even as slavery was beginning, the Spanish colonial administration was nearing its end. As a result of internal rivalries and conflicts and because of the impoverished state of the island's economy, many Spanish families removed to more prosperous colonies such as Cuba or to the American mainland.

■ British Colony

In the 17th century, Spanish hegemony in the Caribbean was challenged by other rising European powers: France, Holland and England. They had little liking for the sharing out of the New World between Spain and Portugal, and as early as 1506 French ships were attacking Spanish ships

Gravestone of a Port Royal
inhabitant who miraculously
survived the earthquake of
1692.
(Jan Stegeman)

Port Royal: pirate capital

The word 'buccaneer' comes from the French *boucan*, the iron grill on
which wandering gangs of deserters and freebooters used to roast meat.
They lived in the forests on the north coast of Hispaniola and on the
nearby island of Tortuga. For the Spaniards, they were a source of
continual harassment and anxiety. Using stolen ships, the buccaneers
controlled the open sea and terrorised all waters and coasts in the
vicinity. Although the buccaneers often behaved like lawless gangs when
they were looting, there were agreements and even a code of honour. The
booty, for example, had to be divided up fairly. If a buccaneer became
disabled he received a fixed sum of money. If he lost his right arm, he was
given 600 pieces-of-eight or six slaves. The loss of a finger was good for
100 pieces-of-eight or one slave.

Around the time that Jamaica became British, the buccaneers were
settling down on the island. The fort which the English had built near Port
Royal to protect the entrance to the Bay of Kingston became their home

port. At first, the English saw their presence as a threat, but during the war with the Dutch, the buccaneers of Port Royal became their allies. The colonial authorities then granted the buccaneers an official licence to attack ships belonging to hostile nations, hence ensuring that the English possessions in the Caribbean were protected.

Port Royal became a 'pirate capital', a flourishing seaport with more than 8,000 inhabitants. The privateers' ships were repaired and provisioned in the shipyards. The warehouses, the brothels and the taverns were always full.

Henry Morgan was the most successful of the privateers. The son of a prosperous farmer from Wales, he found his way via Barbados to the buccaneers of Hispaniola and later to Jamaica. From Port Royal he under-took legendary expeditions against the Spanish towns of Puerto Principe (Cuba) and Porto Bello and Panama City (both in Panama). After an impressive victory at Panama, he received a hero's welcome in Jamaica and the King of England knighted him. Sir Henry Morgan passed his last days as the Deputy Governor of the island. He died in 1688 of dropsy, the consequence of a wild life and a great deal of rum.

On 7 June 1692 Port Royal suffered a severe earthquake. The town was almost totally devastated, and a large section of it disappeared under water. Two thousand people died instantly, a similar number succumbed to the epidemics which followed. The town has never been rebuilt. Popular superstition has it that Port Royal had been punished for its violent and sinful life. Not for nothing had it been notorious as 'the wickedest city in Christendom'. A new settlement was built on the other side of the bay - Kingston.

and settlements in the Caribbean, while in the middle of the 16th century Dutch merchants were already doing business in the region.

In the 17th century, the struggle for power became more intense. English troops undertook expeditions to Jamaica and inflicted heavy losses on the Spanish colonists. After the English had settled in Virginia (North America) and on some of the other Caribbean islands, they laid siege to Jamaica in 1655.

On 10 May 1655 a fleet of 38 ships and 8,000 men appeared in the port of present-day Kingston. Without encountering any resistance worth mentioning, the English troops under Admiral William Penn and General Robert Venables captured the local fort and pushed on to the capital, Spanish Town. It lay deserted. Most of the Spanish inhabitants had set cattle and slaves free and had fled, via the north coast, to Cuba. Frustrated and enraged, the English burned a large part of Spanish Town to the ground.

The British occupation was not, however, entirely without its own set-backs. From the interior the English were attacked by runaway slaves, sometimes led by Spaniards, who sowed death and destruction. In December 1656, 1,600 British colonists had settled in the marshy area near Port Morant; after a few months, as a result of disease and conflict, only 400 remained. Spanish troops later made a vain attempt to recapture Jamaica, but with the Peace of Madrid (1670) Jamaica officially came under British rule.

With Jamaica the British had control of an important bridgehead in the Caribbean. From there they harried Spanish estates, towns and ships throughout the region, usually in alliance with buccaneers – privateers and pirates. Jamaica became the land of buccaneers and pirates, harbouring legendary characters such as Henry Morgan, Bluebeard and Calico Jack Rackham.

Slaves from West Africa Jamaica is small, approximately one-twentieth of the area of Britain, and has 2.5 million inhabitants. In view of its size, Jamaica has a remarkably varied population. The majority have African forebears. They were the slaves who were brought to the island, particularly in the 18th century, in order to do the heavy work on the plantations. Jamaica was at that time the largest producer of sugar in the Caribbean. The growth of sugar production was impressive; in 1673 there were 57 plantations, in 1740 at least 430.

The majority of the slaves came from West Africa. English slave-traders dominated the market. The ships sailed from ports such as Bristol or Liverpool with merchandise to Africa. There the slaves who had been rounded up were loaded and taken across the Atlantic to Jamaica. Kingston was the most important transfer port in the region for the slave trade. From Jamaica the ships sailed with sugar, rum and molasses back to England, thereby completing the 'triangular trade'. The slave and sugar trade brought the planters in Jamaica and the English slavers enormous wealth.

For the slaves, however, it was an appalling ordeal. During the voyage from Africa to the Caribbean, which might last between six and twelve weeks, the chained slaves lay piled up on shelves, alongside and on top of one another. Many did not survive the journey and died from disease or committed suicide. A large number of them were severely weakened on arrival in the port of Kingston, and for this reason slave prices on the market varied enormously. On average the price was between £25 and £75, but there were exceptions. For instance, a register in the old parish of St John records that a price of £330 was paid for a slave called Jimmy, *'a good carpenter'*. On the other hand, one Quamina, *'a good watchman, but with bad legs'* only fetched sixpence.

Of the slaves brought to Jamaica about 5,000 a year stayed on the island. Most were set to work on the land, while a small number had to do domestic work. The work on the land was hard. The strongest slaves cleared the land, planted out and cut the cane or worked at the sugar mill. Strong boys and girls, as well as older slaves, did the weeding. The youngest children tended the young plants and looked after the cattle.

The regime on most of the plantations was merciless, and the slaves were kept down with harsh corporal punishment. A thrashing with the whip was the very least that a slave could expect for disobedience. The amputation of an arm or a leg, and even the death penalty, by way of deterrent, was not uncommon. During the course of time the punishments became less severe. Yet even in 1830, four years before the abolition of slavery, Congo Nancy was condemned to heavy labour for life because she had run away from the Craig Mill plantation in St George.

■ Rebellion and war: the Maroons

During the period of slavery the slaves resisted both actively and passively. Many took refuge over the years in the Jamaican interior. There they joined the descendants of the slaves who had run away during the Spanish era. The runaway slaves were called Maroons from the Spanish word *cimarrón*, meaning 'wild'.

In the year 1678 there is the first mention of a slave uprising. But the first substantial rebellion came in 1690 in the Parish of Clarendon, from where many slaves escaped to the interior, to Cockpit Country. Together with the Maroons already living there, they attacked plantations, set the crops on fire and stole the animals. Their leader was the escaped slave, Cudjoe. This First Maroon War spread across the whole of the country and was to last many decades (1690-1739). The British troops faced an 'invisible' enemy. The Maroons knew the area much better than the British and they used guerrilla tactics, attacking the enemy in small groups and always in different places.

The tide turned when hunting dogs were brought in to track them down and when Indians from the Mosquito Coast (in present-day Nicaragua and Honduras) and free slaves were paid to join in on the British side. The British won an important victory with the capture and destruction of Nanny Town in the Blue Mountains, named after the leader of the rebels, a black woman called Queen Nanny, who led the Maroons from the remote interior.

The First Maroon War ended in 1739, when the British commanding officer, Colonel Guthrie succeeded in persuading Cudjoe to make peace. Sitting under a large cotton-tree in Cockpit Country, they agreed that the Maroons would be given complete freedom and land of their own in Cockpit Country. The Maroons were allowed to hunt wild pigs anywhere *'outside a three-mile zone around plantations and towns'* and were to have their own jurisdiction. For their part, the Maroons had to desist from

Devon House, in Kingston, the former residence of a plantation owner.
(Jan Stegeman)

attacking the plantations and the colonists, and were not allowed to take in any further escaped slaves. In fact, they had to help the British to track down any such slaves. A year later, a similar treaty was also concluded with the Maroons in the Blue Mountains.

Fifty years of peace   For more than fifty years the peace held. There was, however, one violent interruption. In 1760 a great slave rebellion broke out in St Mary, led by the runaway slave, Tacky. The insurrection began with an attack on the fort in Port Maria and developed into a wave of small uprisings throughout the whole of the island. Tacky took to the mountains with his small but growing army, but there they received no support from the Maroons. Instead, with their assistance, as had been agreed in the peace treaty, the colonial authorities were able to restore order after a few months.

In 1795 two Maroons from Trelawny were publicly whipped, thereby sparking off the Second Maroon War which was to last for five months. The affair was too much for the Maroons of Trelawny, particularly as the man wielding the lash was a slave who had been captured by them and brought back to the plantation. Feeling deceived by the colonial authorities, they were out for revenge. Tensions came to boiling point when a few Maroon chiefs, who were on the way to Spanish Town to air their grievances, were taken captive. The British administration declared a state of siege, and the Maroons were called upon to give themselves up.

A small group did surrender and were promptly taken prisoner. In their anger, the others burned Trelawny Town to the ground and took refuge in the hills, where they laid an ambush for the British soldiers. The war had begun. The British troops obtained help from Maroons from other settlements, and using bloodhounds, began to get the upper hand. Terrified, the rebel Maroons gave themselves up. Practically the whole group from Trelawny Town was banished to Nova Scotia (now a province of Canada). A large number eventually finished up in Sierra Leone in Africa.

Abolition of slavery   With their declaration of a state of siege and the arrests, the British administrators had overreacted to the tensions among the Maroons. This response was generally symptomatic of the fear that colonial society would be undermined by the very institution – slavery – which sustained it. At home in England, meanwhile, more and more prominent citizens were becoming convinced of the unChristian nature of slavery. The abolitionists were to be found in Methodist and Quaker circles but also among free-thinkers and liberals of all persuasions. They provided detailed documentation of the inhuman treatment meted out to the slaves. Through a long propaganda campaign, they won over influential politicians to their side, eventually leading to the prohibition of the slave trade in 1808.

Yet the greatest threat to the planters came from the slaves themselves. In Saint Domingue, the French sector of the neighbouring island of Hispaniola, the fat was already in the fire. Led by Toussaint Louverture, the slaves had themselves succeeded in gaining control of large sections of the colony. French planters who had taken flight brought the news of events in Saint Domingue to the other islands. British and Spanish troops both attempted to mount armed interventions and Napoleon Bonaparte sent a task-force of 22,000 French troops, but the slaves were victorious. In 1804 Haiti was proclaimed the world's first independent black republic.

The example of Haiti inspired many slaves to take up arms and a wave of uprisings swept across the Caribbean. In Jamaica the Baptist preacher Samuel Sharpe was the ringleader of what was to become the last great slave rebellion on the island in 1831. The insurgency lasted five months, with enormous damage to plantations and dwellings. The rebels were severely punished, and Sam Sharpe was hanged in Montego Bay. *'Rather death than life as a slave'* were his last words on the scaffold.

In 1834 slavery was brought to an end. But for another four years the slaves had to work forty hours a week for their masters for no pay. Only then, in 1838, was slavery officially abolished in Jamaica.

New immigrants   Most slaves worked in sugar production. Without their cheap labour, the sugar industry soon began to go downhill, and the planters looked for alternatives. In 1834 a group of German workers arrived from Bremen. In the years that followed further immigrant workers came from Germany, Scotland and Ireland. But this labour system was unsuccessful. Tropical diseases took their toll among the newcomers, many opted for a new existence outside the plantation and a number of them left the island. Only the names of certain places and areas – Hanover, Berlin, Newcastle and Little London – still recall the presence of these European immigrants. And today, on the south coast of St Elizabeth some family names and blue eyes still betray Scottish or Irish origins.

One unusual presence in the population, and a living proof of European immigration following the abolition of slavery, are the *Germaicans*. For generations they have been trying to survive in Seaford Town, a small community in the Westmoreland interior; among the family names are the Kamekas, the Eldermeyers, the Wedermeyers. Some 150 inhabitants of Seaford Town are directly descended from the adventurers who thought that in the Jamaica of the 1830s they had found the land of unbounded opportunity. In the event, it was a bitter disappointment. They were given poor land and could scarcely survive from subsistence farming. They became the 'poor whites' of the island, living off small-scale production of bananas, yams, ginger, cocoa and cassava.

A more successful immigrant community was made up of Asians, who took the place of the slaves. In the period 1838-1917, about 33,000 Indians emigrated to Jamaica and between 1860 and 1893 almost 5,000 Chinese arrived. The Asians were recruited as contract or indentured labourers, working for fixed periods in return for cash or land. Today they are to be found in agriculture, trade, the liberal professions and in government.

Towards the end of the 19th century, another attempt was made to bring over new groups of Africans to the plantations, this time as contract labourers. Some 7,500 braved the crossing. A few claimed their free passage home on the expiry of the contract period, but by far the majority remained and mixed with the other population groups. From the Middle East, especially present-day Lebanon, came other immigrants who engaged principally in trade. In Jamaica they are generally known as 'Syrians'.

■ Crown Colony

In spite of all attempts to provide the plantation with new sources of labour, sugar production went into decline following the abolition of slavery. The contract labourers preferred to start up farming on their own account or they moved to the town once the contract period was over. All over the island new settlements of ex-slaves or ex-contract labourers sprang up, forming a free, but marginalised, peasantry. They often finished up with the least fertile land, marking the beginning of the island's hard-pressed smallholder farming.

The death blow for sugar production was dealt by much higher production costs (there were now wages to be paid) and lower prices on the world market. Also, as a result of the Sugar Equalisation Act of 1846, which removed all protective measures on imports into England, Jamaican sugar was no longer able to compete with the much cheaper sugar exported from Cuba and Brazil, where slavery had not yet been abolished. Traders went bankrupt, and a large section of the planter class was ruined.

A report by the Scottish Presbyterian Pastor John King, who visited the island during this period, shows how desolate the once rich plantation colony had become. *'Everywhere neglected fields, crumbling buildings and rusting machinery...trees were growing through the windows and roofs of the plantation buildings. Even Kingston, the new capital, presented a picture of decay. A section of the town had suffered damage by fire but because of the crisis nothing could be rebuilt. Other parts of the town were no longer being maintained...'*

The political situation was equally dismal. Society might have changed, but the 'plantocracy', the white plantation owners, clung on grimly to power. From 1662 onwards power in Jamaica was in the hands of a British governor and a council appointed by him in consultation with an executive council consisting of the leading white planters.

But since the capture of the island from the Spaniards, the composition of the population had completely changed. Whereas on the eve of its first civil administration there were more than 4,000, mostly white, inhabitants, in 1775 the population numbered 13,000 white and more than 200,000 black Jamaicans. By 1850 Jamaica had a good 300,000 black inhabitants, former slaves and their children. In law they were free, but they were excluded from politics as they had no vote and could not be elected. For a long time the exclusion also applied to the mulattos, but they were given the vote in 1830.

Compared with the ex-slaves, the mulattos, descendants of planters and slave women, had the advantage of being protected by their fathers and obtaining their freedom earlier. They found their way into the liberal professions, business life and the military, and some even acquired a respectable piece of land. Most of the mulattos, once they had obtained the right to vote, lined up on the side of the white elite and supported all the measures designed to deny the black population its rights. For instance, in 1834 and 1836 laws were adopted whereby the right to vote was linked to

SAM SHARPE   Paul Bogle   George William Gordon

income and property, a measure which ensured that the former slaves were excluded. There were also, however, mulattos such as George William Gordon, who chose the side of the ex-slaves. Gordon was a successful businessman in Kingston and had sat in the parliament since 1850. Active in society, politics and commerce, he represented the aspiring mulatto middle class but also consistently spoke up for the position of the black smallholders.

The Morant Bay Rebellion   In the 1860s resentment was brewing among the black population against the authorities who were denying them land and political rights. There was also discontent over low wages, high levels of unemployment and the escalating prices of food. One of the black spokes-men was Paul Bogle, the son of an ex-slave and a deacon in the Baptist Church. A lawsuit against one of Paul Bogle's followers was the overture to the infamous Morant Bay Rebellion of 1865.

During the trial, which took place in Morant Bay, fighting broke out between Bogle's supporters and the authorities around the courthouse. The authorities held Bogle responsible and issued a warrant for his arrest and for the arrest of some of his followers. But Bogle's fellow workers over-powered the police patrol which came to arrest them and they organised a march on the town. On the way the group swelled in numbers, and by the time the protestors reached Morant Bay, a full-scale riot was inevitable. The police station was attacked, weapons were seized and shops looted. Dozens of people were killed, at first among the demonstrators and the police, and later on among white planters who were murdered in the surge of rage. By way of reprisal, the authorities had 430 rebels executed, 600 were flogged and a thousand houses were burned to the ground. Paul Bogle was hanged. Even George William Gordon, who was held to be the instigator of the insurrection, was sentenced to the gallows.

The rebellion had far-reaching consequences. A royal commission of investigation sent to the island concluded that the old administrative structures should disappear. Jamaica became a crown colony: the parliament was sent packing and the island came under the direct rule of the British crown, enabling the implementation of reforms in administration and legislation. The old local elite was no longer able to block every reform and found its traditional authority severely reduced. Education, healthcare and the infrastructure were improved, and in the economy bananas gradually and partially took the place of sugar. Until the 1930s, Jamaica remained relatively peaceful.

2   POLITICS

Lost illusions

Around 1940 the foundation was laid for the present political system. For over sixty years Jamaica had been a crown colony. Although the crown colony administration was at the time an improvement compared with the old 'plantocracy', sooner or later the limitations of this form of government had to become obvious. Beneath the surface, resistance was brewing against the paternalistic type of government and against the Legislative Council, consisting of the Governor, nine appointed and nine elected members. In general, the local population had hardly any influence on policy. The number of black representatives had, however, in a short space of time increased considerably: in 1920 they formed a majority in the Legislative Council. A number of black Jamaicans were also to be found in the government offices. But when it came to decisions, it was the opinion of the Governor, supported by his nine appointed members, which inevitably carried the day.

■ Trade unions and political parties

The worldwide depression, which began in 1929 in the United States and Britain, dragged Jamaica down with it. Sugar production had already fallen substantially because of fierce competition from sugar-beet in Europe. Now banana exports were also falling. Emigration was no longer a possibility as practically everywhere, countries were tightening restrictions.

The island's population had increased sharply. Wages were low, the level of unemployment was high and the colonial government was in no position to lend a helping hand. This intolerable situation applied to all the British colonies in the Caribbean. A wave of strikes and riots passed across the region (St Kitts, Barbados, Trinidad, St Vincent and St Lucia) which gave rise to the establishment of trade unions and political parties.

The year 1938 was crucial for Jamaica. A strike at the West Indies Sugar Company in the township of Frome in Westmoreland got out of hand. During a confrontation with armed police, some strikers were killed and several dozen wounded. This incident was followed by protests, strikes and looting all over the island. Amidst this volatile series of developments the Bustamante Industrial Trade Union (BITU) was set up bearing the name of the most important strike leader of the moment, Alexander Bustamante. The BITU was the first trade union in the whole of the Caribbean. In that same year, the lawyer Norman Washington Manley (father of the later prime minister, Michael Manley) formed the first political party in Jamaica, the People's National Party (PNP).

These new leaders appearing on the national stage stood for improving the position of the workers and for political reforms. A royal commission of enquiry under Lord Moyne reached similar recommendations in its report of 1945. The Second World War also brought some progress in its wake. The islands in the Caribbean became important Allied bases, and contributed to the supply of food, fuel and essential raw materials for the war economy. This was reason enough for the British government substantially to increase financial subsidies to the Caribbean colonies. In 1942 the Anglo-American Caribbean Commission was set up, in which France and the Netherlands, with their own colonies in the region, also participated at a later stage. This organisation was to establish a framework for the economic and social development in the region.

In 1944 Jamaica was given a new constitution. This provided for an elected government on the basis of universal suffrage, a move strongly campaigned for by Norman Manley. After years of political organising, the leader of the PNP and his party had ensured a broad base within the population for self-government.

Parting of the ways   Norman Manley and the trade union leader Alexander Bustamante, although at first of one mind, were eventually to pursue separate political goals. In 1943 Bustamante had set up his own party, the Jamaica Labour Party (JLP). As a result, a second large trade union organisation was founded as an extension to Norman Manley's PNP, the Trade Union Congress (TUC). These organisations laid the foundation for Jamaica's present-day political system.

Under Bustamante's leadership, the JLP developed into a party with a liberal and capitalist ideology, while little by little, Manley and his PNP leant more towards socialism though deeply influenced by nationalist and Christian thinking. The first elections in 1944 were won by the JLP. The slogan 'Bread and Butter' appealed to the population at this time rather more than matters of independence which the PNP championed vociferously. The next elections in 1949 were again won by the JLP.

In 1955 the PNP took over the helm and under Manley's leadership, Jamaica progressed on the road to independence. That independence needed to be forged, according to Manley, in the form of a federal constitution. This belief was based on the notion that the British islands in the Caribbean were too small to make any progress entirely by themselves and that there would need to remain a strong mutual bond. For this reason the West Indies Federation was established in 1958.

Norman Manley and Alexander
Bustamante signing the Treaty of
Independence in 1962.
(Spaarnestad Fotoarchief)

■ The federal experiment

The British West Indies consisted of dozens of islands and two regions on
the mainland. In terms of present-day states they comprised: Jamaica, the
British Virgin Islands, Anguilla, Antigua and Barbuda, St Kitts-Nevis,
Montserrat, Dominica, St Vincent and the Grenadines, St Lucia, Barbados,
Grenada, Trinidad and Tobago, the Cayman Islands, the Bahamas, the
Turks and Caicos Islands and on the mainland Belize (then British
Honduras) and Guyana. The population of this area in about 1960 was
some 3.2 million inhabitants. In 1990 it was 5.8 million, of which 2.4
million (41%) lived in Jamaica. The other 'great powers' were Trinidad
and Tobago with 1.2 million and Guyana with 0.8 million.

The British government and the new generation of political leaders in
the region shared the view that the independence of small and isolated
states had to be discouraged. Combining strengths in a federal structure
was the only way to create sufficient economic potential and a domestic
market of any size. *'It is impossible to assume that each island, even the
largest, could by itself be in a position to provide the basic necessities of a
modern state'*, said Norman Manley in Montego Bay in March 1945.

The British administrators had already made attempts to bring individual islands together to form a federation but these attempts had always met with reluctance on the part of most islanders who were more concerned with their own individual territories and entertained a great deal of suspicion towards the inhabitants of the neighbouring islands.

After the war it did seem that the time was ripe for a federation. Links and communication between the islands were improving and cautious initial steps were made towards collaboration, such as the scheme to set up a joint university. In 1953 the first plan for a West Indies Federation was presented. Government was to be exercised by an Upper House and a Lower House. The members of the Upper House would be appointed by the Governor-General, while the members of the Lower House would be elected. Seventeen seats would go to Jamaica, Trinidad and Tobago would together be allocated ten, Barbados five, St Kitts-Nevis, Anguilla, Antigua, Dominica, St Lucia, St Vincent and Grenada two each and Montserrat one.

Islands going it alone   At the same time, however, during the 1940s and 1950s there were forces developing in the opposite direction. One by one, the British colonies were beginning to stand on their own feet. The larger islands, Jamaica, Trinidad and Barbados, obtained universal suffrage and a certain amount of self-rule. In Jamaica and Trinidad the economies grew at an unprecedented rate through the production of bauxite and oil respectively.

The economic success of these islands undermined the political consensus on federation. The large islands were afraid that they would have to subsidise the development of their smaller and weaker brethren and the general opinion in Trinidad and Jamaica was that the other islands should also make out by their own efforts. Nevertheless, the federation had its official start on 3 January 1958. But it was the rivalry between the two prominent countries, Jamaica and Trinidad, that would prove to be the time-bomb beneath the federation.

Port of Spain (Trinidad) became the federal capital, where on 22 April 1958 the first session of the West Indian parliament took place. The Premier was Grantley Adams, the prime minister of Barbados. In fact, it was a very hollow federation, having a federal cabinet without real power and a structure in which the self-interest of the large islands predominated. The best illustration of this lack of federal spirit was the attempt by the Jamaicans to set up their own refinery which would compete directly with Trinidad's oil industry. The federation threatened to impose sanctions on Jamaica and tensions ran high. Yet Jamaica continued to put its own interests first, insisting that in no way could its economic interests be damaged by the federal structure. The Jamaicans attempted to reduce even further the federation's authority in economic policy and at the same time wanted more seats in the federal parliament. The dispute became 'Jamaica versus the rest' and the rest were led by Trinidad.

The final hour of the West Indies Federation struck in 1960. Alexander Bustamante spoke out against the federation expressing his view that Jamaica should withdraw from membership. He himself resigned as leader of the Federal Democratic Labour Party (FDLP). Prime Minister Norman Manley placed the decision in the hands of the people and an overwhelming 'no' in the referendum on 19 September 1961 sealed the fate of the West Indies Federation. After its disintegration all the former British colonies went their own way. Since then most have become independent states with their own seats in the UN. A few are still British possessions.

Independence   In the wake of the Federation's collapse, the British government swiftly gave its consent to Jamaican independence. On the evening of 5 August 1962 a grand celebration in the National Stadium in Kingston inaugurated independence. At midnight the Union Jack was lowered for the last time and the black, green and gold of the new national flag was raised. Jamaica became an independent state within the British Commonwealth.

The Jamaican parliament has a House of Representatives with sixty seats and a Senate with 21 seats. The representatives are elected by a simple majority or 'first past the post' system in the fourteen parishes. The Queen is represented in Jamaica by a Governor-General. The latter has mainly a ceremonial function and is appointed on the recommendation of the Jamaican prime minister. The prime minister likewise appoints thirteen members of the Senate, while the remaining eight members are appointed in consultation with the leader of the opposition.

■ The PNP and democratic socialism

From their very start the PNP and the JLP fought each other for political power. The founders of the two parties, Norman Manley and Alexander Bustamante, initially differed mainly in their views on the speed of the move to self-rule. After independence the two parties grew ideologically even further away from each other. The JLP oriented itself towards the West, especially the United States, and was an advocate of a liberal economic policy. *'I'm with the West, I'm against communism'* was the slogan with which Prime Minister Bustamante set the course after independence. It was a time of relative prosperity through the expansion of industry. Large foreign investments took place, particularly in the mining and initial processing of bauxite.

The PNP increasingly adapted to a radical form of social democracy, 'socialism with a human face', which the party usually referred to as 'democratic socialism'. When between 1972-1980 a PNP government under Norman Manley's son Michael was in power, this policy was put into practice, as the PNP tried to broaden the economic base of the country by means of greater government control and social reforms. Manley proclaimed his message with slogans such as *'Better must come'* and *'Power for the people'*. With his charismatic personality and fiery rhetoric, he managed to win over a large number of Jamaicans to his policies. In progressive circles in other countries, both western and developing, Manley also commanded respect with his radical positions on national and international issues.

People's projects   During his first term Michael Manley honoured a number of election promises, introducing a statutory minimum wage and new labour legislation. A start was made with the distribution of land in favour of the small farmers and credit facilities for this sector were extended. Reforms made education and healthcare more accessible and the government initiated a literacy campaign. The PNP administration also supported the building of more public-sector housing and encouraged a greater degree of democratic participation at the local level.

All these people's projects, as they were called, had to be financed by a greater government control of vital economic sectors and this brought Michael Manley into direct conflict with the international business world. The affair of the bauxite levies was perhaps the most crucial conflict. Manley wanted to increase the tax paid by foreign multinationals involved with bauxite extraction and processing and he wanted the government to have a majority share in these industries. When negotiations with the transnational aluminium companies failed, the government unilaterally imposed higher taxes. Within one year the effect was nullified when the companies drastically reduced their bauxite mining while at the same time Jamaica's oil bill tripled because of the 1973-4 oil crisis.

Cuba   Manley also carried through innovations in foreign policy. Jamaica forged close ties with its socialist neighbour Cuba and became a prominent participant in the Non-aligned Movement. Michael Manley was one of the pioneers in the debate on North-South relations, expressing radical ideas on the relationship between the rich 'centre' and poor 'periphery' of world trade and power.

The popularity which Manley enjoyed in progressive circles was not to be found among Jamaicans from the middle and higher income groups. Higher taxes, increasing influence of government in society and left-wing rhetoric ensured disquiet in this part of Jamaican society. The conservative *Daily Gleaner*, by far the largest daily newspaper in Jamaica, stirred the discontent by drawing attention to the presence in Jamaica of doctors, teachers and other experts from Cuba. A fair number of Jamaicans with money left the country and settled in Canada and the United States; others transferred their capital to banks abroad.

Michael Manley's social programmes aimed to improve the
island's often poor housing

conditions. Rural housing near
St Ann's Bay.
(Jan Stegemen)

Political patronage

In Jamaica, politics means the PNP and the JLP. This goes hand in hand with
a whole tradition of rhetoric and loyalty which comes to the point of
hysteria during election time. Both parties have strong connections with
pressure groups in society, such as trade unions, the media and the
employers. A system of political patronage ensures that the link is
maintained. As a reward for support and assistance during elections, loyal
supporters of the winning party can count on privileges such as contracts,
work and housing. It is not unusual for loyal party supporters to be
appointed to a whole variety of posts in ministries and other government
organisations immediately following the elections.

The influence of partisan politics on daily life is almost palpable in the
slum districts of Kingston. Downtown Kingston is divided up into PNP and
JLP districts or 'garrisons'. Militant supporters of the two parties rule the
roost in their own power bases. For them, the bond with the party is a
matter of life or death. Hundreds of people met their death here in the
election campaigns of 1976 and 1980. The slogans on the walls 'JLP war
zone', 'You are entering PNP city' speak for themselves.

The JLP, under its new leader, Edward Seaga, formed the opposition. Under Seaga's leadership the JLP presented itself as fiercely anti-communist, as the party of the free market and democracy. Seaga accused Manley of wanting to reshape Jamaica to become a one-party state on the model of Cuba.

The 1976 elections were held in an atmosphere of intense political polarisation. Violence escalated in the run-up to the polling and in the slum districts of Kingston the political campaigns assumed the form of a war. Heavily armed gangs of PNP and JLP supporters attacked each other while the politicians fanned the flames with accusations of secret support from abroad. According to the JLP, PNP-supporters were obtaining weapons from Cuba, whereas in the actions of the JLP the PNP, with some justification, saw the hand of the CIA.

In an attempt to stem the violence, Prime Minister Manley declared a state of emergency and gave the police and judiciary additional powers including the establishment of the so-called Gun Court, a prison and non-jury court for violent offenders. With the aid of summary justice, the denial of bail and severe sentencing the government managed to clamp down on political violence. In judicial circles Manley's measures were criticised as a violation of basic human rights. But for the time being, at least, the violence abated. The PNP won the elections and obtained 47 of the sixty seats.

Manley interpreted the election result as a mandate to press on with his democratic-socialist policies. This led to further confrontation with political and economic forces at home and abroad. The Jamaican government found it more and more difficult to obtain capital as foreign financial institutions and investors kept away from the island. The ties with Cuba and the Jamaican support for the Cuban intervention in Angola were thorns in the flesh of the US government. It, in return, stepped up pressure on Manley's government with a series of economic sanctions.

Retrenchment policies   In the meantime capital flight and economic stagnation made it more and more difficult for Manley to finance his social programmes. At home there were too few resources, and it was becoming increasingly difficult to attract foreign loans. Eventually, Jamaica ran into problems with the International Monetary Fund (IMF) to which it was forced to turn for balance-of-payments support. In 1977 and 1978 an agreement was concluded in respect of new credits in which Manley had to implement a tight policy of retrenchment including public sector cuts and the removal of many social programmes. When, after two years, scarcely any improvement had been achieved, the Jamaican government broke with the IMF. It was a sensational decision. According to Manley, a new IMF package of austerity measures would result in an unacceptable lowering of the standard of living. It was politically unacceptable not least because the 1980 elections were by now around the corner.

During Manley's second term of office the economic chaos and political polarisation increased and the violence spread. The year 1980 entered history as the island's most violent since the Morant Bay Rebellion of 1865. Hundreds of people died in street fights and gang attacks, among them being 167 old women who lost their lives in an arson attack on a poorhouse in Kingston. The so-called 'garrison' constituencies of Kingston were ruled by party vigilantes. Edward Seaga's JLP won the elections, promising 'deliverance' and revival of the collapsed economy. The result was a political landslide in which the JLP obtained 51 out of the sixty seats.

The JLP and the free West

As Edward Seaga entered office as the new prime minister, Jamaica once more aligned itself with the 'free West' camp. Diplomatic links with Cuba were severed. Immediately after his election victory, Seaga paid a visit to the new US president, Ronald Reagan, one of the first foreign leaders to do so. Two years later in 1982, Reagan paid an official return visit with the object of demonstrating his support for Seaga's policies.

Seaga was an outspoken supporter of the Caribbean Basin Initiative (CBI) launched by the Reagan administration as a means of countering the growing influence of radical regimes in the region. By extending export opportunities to the US, investment and employment in the region were to be stimulated. In exchange, the Americans expected that the governments concerned would observe the democratic rules by holding free elections and respecting human rights.

Some political leaders in the region experienced considerable difficulty with this politically slanted economic development programme. Not so Seaga; under his leadership during the 1980s Jamaica became more or less the opposite pole to the socialist and communist oriented countries such as Nicaragua, Grenada and, of course, Cuba. In 1982 Seaga even tried to oust Grenada from CARICOM, the Caribbean Common Market. Jamaica's participation in the invasion of Grenada was likewise a clear indication of Seaga's political attitude.

Loyal ally   In October 1983 US troops, supported by special units from Jamaica and a few East Caribbean islands, put an end to the short-lived communist regime in Grenada. Four years before, a peaceful revolution had taken place in Grenada, but in the autumn of 1983 the revolution had been derailed when the moderate socialist prime minister, Maurice Bishop, together with some hundred of his supporters, was murdered in cold blood by hardline Marxists. The bloodbath shook the whole region and the *Daily Gleaner* immediately blamed Cuba. Referring to the Manley period, the newspaper commented that *'That could also have happened in Jamaica'*.

Seaga, whose popularity had already waned to a considerable extent because of the severe retrenchment policy, deftly turned the invasion to his political advantage and brought the elections forward by one year. In protest, particularly against the fact that the new electors' lists were not ready, the PNP decided to boycott the elections. The consequence was that from 1983 to 1989 not only did Jamaica have a one-party government but also a one-party parliament. The PNP conducted its opposition outside parliament, organising mass meetings at which political issues were discussed and criticism was levelled at JLP policy.

During the 1980s Jamaica was effectively tied to the IMF's apron strings as Seaga kept to the economic restructuring programme in exemplary fashion. The prime minister enjoyed supreme power since he was not only prime minister but at the same time also minister for finance and planning, information, culture and defence. Seaga loved solo appearances; with him at the helm Jamaican politics became a one-man show. More and more Jamaicans were disturbed by this cult of personality. Added to this was the high price which poor Jamaicans were having to pay for Seaga's policies and persistent rumours of corruption in government circles. The cost of living rose while unemployment and poverty grew.

But Seaga showed his best side after Hurricane Gilbert had devastated the island in September 1988. He took the leading role in the rescue programme and managed to obtain huge sums of money for restoration from aid organisations and friendly governments.

■ A new era

Seaga's economic recovery policy cost him his popularity. At the 1989 elections, Michael Manley and the PNP scored a resounding win. It was his third period of office and his 'second chance' as he himself called it. During the election campaign the 'Cuba' theme played a large part. Would Manley go back to the former socialist model? The socialist leader proved to have changed during his nine years in the political wilderness. The socialist rhetoric had disappeared and the issue now was continuity in policy and consensus in society. He would pursue a social policy, he insisted, but on the basis of a free-market philosophy.

Six months before the elections, Seaga and Manley had concluded a sort of peace treaty in order as far as possible to avoid political violence. It worked. The elections were a picture of peace and order, at least in comparison with the turbulent years 1976 and 1980. 'Only' thirteen lost their lives.

Immediately following his victory, Manley let it be known that he intended to establish contact with US President George Bush. He stressed the importance of the Enterprise for the Americas Initiative, a plan similar

Prime Minister Percival
J. Patterson.
(Foto: AP)

to President Reagan's Caribbean Basin Initiative. Through *rapprochment* Manley hoped to be able to gain benefits in the sphere of investments, trade and debt relief. This time, even under Manley, Jamaica kept up with the demands of the IMF and the World Bank, gradually liberalising key sectors of the economy. But in 1990 he did restore diplomatic relations with Cuba, stating as his reason the fact that Jamaica wished to sail an independent political course. He also strengthened ties with other, non-English-speaking, countries in the region such as Mexico and Venezuela, while at the same time, Jamaica continued to play a leading role in CARICOM, in which Seaga had never been very interested.

Prime Minister Patterson   For reasons of health Michael Manley was unable to complete his third term of office and at the beginning of 1992 he handed over the premiership to the lawyer and party chairman, Percival J. Patterson. The new prime minister of Jamaica was a much less charismatic figure than the two traditional adversaries, Michael Manley and Edward Seaga. Patterson continued with the moderately liberal policy of Manley and he made a start on privatising some 300 'unproductive' government agencies and public enterprises.

Slowly Patterson made himself popular, primarily by his low-key manner of conducting politics. For instance, he proposed to deal with major problems in conjunction with the opposition and a joint plan to combat crime was produced. For the first time it was to be not only the street fighters but also the white-collar criminals who would be prosecuted. He also gained popularity with his public appearances, making sure he was to be seen regularly at sports functions and music festivals. Most significantly, Patterson was that rarity – a black politician – in an island traditionally dominated by light-skinned dynastic families such as the Manleys.

Backed by favourable opinion poll results, Patterson ventured to call new elections for March 1993. He came through with flying colours as the PNP won 53 of the sixty seats. The turnout was low and the campaign was violent again; in the days around the elections twelve people were killed and dozens injured in a series of gun-fights.

The defeated JLP leader Seaga hinted that he would quit politics but to date still remains the leader of the JLP and the official opposition. Never had the JLP suffered such a shattering defeat. (*'Have mercy Percy'* was the succinct newspaper headline). And so came to an end a period of a quarter of a century in which two men, Edward Seaga and his constant rival Michael Manley, determined political policy. A new era is now perhaps dawning in Jamaican politics. Prime Minister Patterson promised after his election victory that the age of political confrontation was over. With the confidence of the electorate, he said, he would begin working 'for a more peaceful and a more productive Jamaica'.

3 THE ECONOMY

Rich but vulnerable

_____ *'Jamaica is in the position of a drowning man, treading water to keep afloat, but slowly drifting offshore.'* Professor Kari Levitt, University of the West Indies, Jamaica.

■ Debts and dependence

Jamaica has become dependent on foreign credits. Time and again, the island has to plead with the donor countries and international financial institutions for rescheduling of old debts and the granting of new loans. When the US government announced in August 1991 that Jamaica's outstanding bilateral debt had been 'forgiven', the authorities in Kingston could not contain their delight. Prime Minister Michael Manley called it a 'historic act'. Other donor countries such as Canada, Great Britain, Germany, Japan and the Netherlands have in recent years either done the same or have deferred repayment of interest and capital due. This has given Jamaica some relief, but only temporarily. The largest burden of debt, to the IMF and the World Bank, still exists and has to be repaid in regular installments.

Financial stranglehold At the beginning of 1993 Jamaica's foreign debts amounted to a total of US$4.5 billion. For a relatively small economy this is an enormous burden. This debt, calculated per head of the population (about US$1,800) and as a percentage of gross national product (132 per cent), is one of the highest in the world. A good forty per cent of foreign currency earnings are used annually to meet capital and interest commitments. Every year Jamaica pays back to international financiers more than it receives in new loans and gifts.

The debt has a profound impact on society. The stranglehold of the debt burden forces cuts in in government expenditure and imports of basic commodities. The general cost-of-living index has shot up, affecting most seriously the poorest Jamaicans. In 1979 the minimum wage was 26 Jamaican dollars and the cost of maintaining a family of five was calculated at about 24 dollars; in 1992 the minimum weekly wage was 120 dollars and the average cost of living 250 dollars.

For the unemployed, estimated in 1992 at thirty per cent of the economically active population, the situation is desperate. With a bit of scratching around in the informal sector, many unemployed try to scrape up a meagre income, but casual, irregular and badly paid work cannot keep pace with the rapidly rising cost of living. At the moment, one in three households is living below the poverty line. The population is also hard hit by lack of healthcare, education, housing programmes and public transport.

A dependent economy   The economic problems with which Jamaica is wrestling result to a significant extent from the open, dependent and therefore very vulnerable nature of the economy.

A considerable part of gross national product (GNP) goes on foreign trade. The economy is heavily dependent on imports of raw materials (oil) and component parts as well as technology, capital, management and various kinds of consumer goods. Imports must be paid for with the returns from tourism and exports of bauxite, sugar and bananas.

Nevertheless, in the last fifty years the base of the economy has been broadened to a considerable extent. Far more than in the days of the plantations, the riches provided by nature and the soil are being put to use. Particularly during the Second World War and in the first ten years of independence Jamaica, economically speaking, was booming. The island rapidly became one of the world's most important producers of bauxite, as the bauxite alumina industry underwent expansion on a massive scale in order to supply the aircraft industry during the war and later on to provide for the needs of the growing civil aviation industry. In that period, GNP grew by an average of seven per cent per year. The most spectacular increase occurred in the first half of the 1950s, with an average increase of ten per cent per year. The bauxite sector grew in a period of thirty years (1940-1970) from practically nothing to represent 12.5 per cent of GNP. Other growth areas were construction, industry and tourism.

Import substitution activity   Up until 1972 the Jamaican government stimulated economic activity on the basis of a strategy of 'industrialisation by invitation'. Industrial concerns, particularly North American companies, were invited to set up subsidiary companies and were able to profit from low wages and highly attractive investment regulations. Companies in the textiles and leather industries, in particular, were established on the island, with their manufactures aimed at foreign markets.

Companies were also set up which tried to reduce the need to import, a strategy known as import substitution. Most of these import substitution companies produced foodstuffs and basic consumer goods, but domestic producers also manufactured telephones, television sets, and metal and plastic products.

In the course of the 1960s and at the beginning of the 1970s Jamaica became an increasingly popular tourist destination, as prosperity in the countries of the West and the fall in long-haul air fares made intercontinental journeys possible. With an influx of visitors from the US, Canada and Europe, tourism became the second largest source of income after bauxite.

Agriculture has always been important. At the beginning of the 1970s a quarter of the population was still directly or indirectly dependent on sugar-cane production. The production of cocoa, bananas, coffee, citrus fruits, tobacco and coconut provided employment for a large number of rural Jamaicans. The agricultural sector in 1972 accounted for about half the proceeds from exports. (Twenty years later this had become a mere twenty per cent).

But the period of economic growth did not bring about any reduction in social problems. Partly because of the growth in population, the level of unemployment remained very high, and in spite of the broadening of its base, the economy remained vulnerable. Dependence upon agricultural exports was exchanged for dependence on bauxite and tourism. Worse, these were precisely the growth sectors which proved to be most sensitive to fluctuations in global economic trends. In addition, the big bauxite concerns were in foreign hands, which meant that a significant portion of the profits did not remain in Jamaica.

Bauxite, red gold   Since the Second World War Jamaica has earned most of its foreign currency from the extraction and initial processing of bauxite. Bauxite, the raw material of the aluminium industry, is to be found in abundance in the limestone plateau in the interior. The thickness of the seams varies from ten to more than thirty metres. They lie close to the surface, so that open-cast mining is possible.

Bauxite production in Jamaica is in the hands of a few US and Canadian aluminium manufacturers, namely Alcan, Alcoa, Kaiser and Alpart (owned by Kaiser, Reynolds and Atlantic Richfield). Alcoa manages the Clarendon alumina works which are owned by the state.

The companies have concessions which cover vast areas of the interior, and huge sections of the land are kept back in reserve for mining. Only a small part is actually excavated. Lorries with wheels six feet high transport the raw bauxite to the washing and drying plant, where the water content of the red grit is reduced. One part of the purified bauxite is subsequently taken by rail direct to the ports for export. Another part is first processed on the island to make alumina. The final and most profitable stage in the production process from bauxite to aluminium takes place in other countries. This is because there is no cheap energy available in Jamaica and this is essential for aluminium production.

Bauxite mining and processing are vital to Jamaica's economy. Although the bauxite industry can scarcely be said to provide employment – only one per cent of the working population – it does account for half of

Alcan bauxite mining near
Mandeville.
(Michael Kooren)

export earnings and a quarter of government income. In the last few
decades, Jamaica has learned how dangerous it is to be dependent on a
single export. It has also become clear how little room for manoeuvre there
is for a national policy in respect of international bauxite production.
During the turbulent 1970s, with the glaring confrontation between
Manley's socialist government and the transnational mining companies,
the producers drastically reduced their activities, threatening to move to
less troublesome countries such as Brazil and Australia. But in the first
half of the 1980s, after Seaga had taken power, the problems were by no
means over. Production and returns collapsed completely as a result of
world recession and the practically simultaneous opening-up of new mines
in such other countries as Guinea and Australia. Only after 1984 did the
bauxite sector recover to any extent, and in 1992, production of raw
bauxite reached 11.3 million tons. Because of the fall in the price of
aluminium, however, earnings from bauxite remain at a lower level.

National policy   Michael Manley's PNP government of the 1970s attempted to take a
radical new direction in economic planning and policy. With his public
projects, Manley set his sights on the local economy and social development, and the government increased spending on education and healthcare, improved labour legislation and introduced a statutory minimum

wage. The government also tried to extend its grasp on the economy by taking over various foreign companies such as public utilities, sections of the sugar industry, a flour-mill, and a few hotels and banks. Another ambition was to acquire a majority share in Jamaica's bauxite mining and alumina production and to buy back the land under the control of the aluminium producers. In the international sphere, Michael Manley strongly advocated the formation of a cartel of bauxite producers. In the short term, he presented the mining companies with hugely increased levies for the ore they mined.

We have already seen how this policy immediately ran into difficulties and how problems quickly arose with payments. The deficit in the current account grew, foreign investment decreased, capital flight took on unprecedented proportions.

Jamaica and the IMF   *The period 1976-1980 was a traumatic one for Manley's govern-ment. The economy went into decline and unemployment rose rapidly. The government was forced to resort to foreign borrowing just to keep the civil service, education, healthcare and state industries to some extent still operating. Inevitably, Jamaica fell into the vicious circle of loans, debt and repayment.*

As is the case with many other countries in the South, Jamaica has insufficient capital of its own for its development and is heavily dependent on foreign creditors. Very soon after independence the country had already got deeply into debt, encouraged to do so by the willingness by which the international financial world provided credit to developing countries up to the 1981 debt crisis.

The Manley government, because of the acute currency shortage and the great difficulty in finding other foreign creditors, was forced to turn to the IMF, the 'lender of last resort'. In order to be considered for credits, the government had to comply with very strict conditions in respect of economic and social policies. The agreements with the IMF have since been a permanent factor in Jamaica's economy and politics.

In 1977 and 1978 Manley signed two agreements which signalled draconian cuts in government spending. Subsidies on basic foodstuffs and goods were drastically reduced, wages were frozen and the government pressed ahead with restoring private enterprise in sectors which it had nationalised. The economic and social consequences of this policy shift alienated a large section of the PNP rank and file. Equally, because there were no discernible benefits such as more foreign investment or improved terms of trade, the Manley government, with its eye on the immediately forthcoming elections, cancelled the IMF agreements in January 1980. But it was too late to help the PNP.

The new JLP government of Prime Minister Edward Seaga directed its policies entirely towards the restoration of the free market. Close links with the United States were forged, and Jamaica got the lion's share of the Reagan administration's Caribbean Basin Initiative, which stimulated investments in the region by expanding export access to the US. In 1981 a further agreement was concluded with the IMF and the doors were also opened again to other financial institutions.

The international recession   The inflow of foreign capital provided some comfort for the economy, but the international economic recession at the beginning of the 1980s brought fresh problems. The balance of payments deteriorated because of a sharp fall in demand for Jamaican export products, especially bauxite. Once again, the targets set by the IMF appeared in danger of being missed, and the IMF threatened to cut off the loans. In 1984, therefore, the Seaga government decided upon a sweeping programme of reconstruction; once again, drastic cuts, tax rises, devaluation of the Jamaican dollar, and the abolition of price controls and import restrictions meant that the Jamaican economy was wide open.

But even these draconian measures could not right the structural imbalance of the Jamaican economy. Too little was being earned by exports to meet the huge import bill and to pay off the accumulating burden of debt. Even the fall in the price of oil after 1986 scarcely lightened the load.

When in 1989 Michael Manley again took over the helm, even he was obliged to submit to the by now well-known IMF recipes. In February he announced a tough programme of stabilisation with new cuts in social spending, increases in taxes and prices and a wave of privatisation schemes for government offices. In 1992 a start was made with the sale of three hundred loss-making government and parastatal agencies, including the sugar industry and Air Jamaica, the national airline.

■ Means of existence

The economic policies of the last fifteen years have brought about highly fluctuating results. There was a short revival in the period 1981-1983 and in the years between 1986 and 1989. At the beginning of the 1990s, the upward trend continued with annual growth figures of two to three per cent of GNP. The programme of reconstruction and privatisation was helped above all by the favourable climate for foreign investment. The mining sector and tourism made the greatest contribution to the revival, while at the same time the devalued Jamaican dollar stimulated growth in the export-oriented industrial sector. The downside was that a large number of companies which produced for the local market went bankrupt as a result of much cheaper imported consumer goods. As the consequence of tight austerity policies, unemployment continued to rise. Jamaica is now one of the cheapest labour markets in the region.

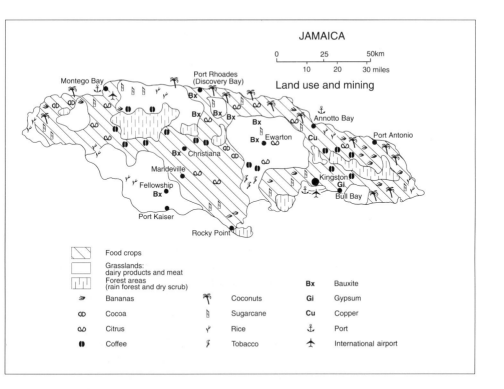

JAMAICA

0   25   50km

10   20   30 miles

Land use and mining

Legend:

- Food crops
- Grasslands: dairy products and meat
- Forest areas (rain forest and dry scrub)
- ⇒ Bananas
- ⊄ Cocoa
- ∞ Citrus
- ❶ Coffee
- 🌴 Coconuts
- 🌾 Sugarcane
- ⫙ Rice
- 🌿 Tobacco
- **Bx** Bauxite
- **Gi** Gypsum
- **Cu** Copper
- ⚓ Port
- ✈ International airport

Agriculture   The basic structure of the Jamaican economy has been changed very little since independence. What keeps the economy afloat is, and will continue to be, the export of bauxite and alumina, a few agricultural products and tourism. The bauxite sector accounts for half of all earnings from exports.

Agriculture, although losing its share of GNP in the last decades, still accounts for one-fifth of the total value of exports. Traditional export crops such as sugar-cane, cocoa, coffee and bananas have not yet entirely surrendered their position. These crops occupy the greatest part of the available agricultural land and provide work for a quarter of a million farmers.

At the beginning of the 1990s sugar-cane production once again exceeded the 200,000 ton level. The bulk of this comes from large plantations, but small and medium-sized businesses produce between thirty and forty per cent of sugar-cane, which they then supply to the factories on the plantations. Productivity in the sugar industry is low because of outdated machinery and inefficient management.

Unlike sugar-cane, banana production is rather more in the hands of small farmers. Bananas are, however, highly prone to disease and extremes of weather conditions. Hurricanes Allen (1980) and Gilbert (1988) dealt banana production a heavy blow, from which it has not yet fully recovered.

Ganja, the holy herb

The small farmer in Jamaica has also become the victim of crisis policies. Together with small businesses in trade and industry, the thousands of smallholdings form the backbone of the local economy. They are of great importance for the local food supply, they operate for the most part with local materials and products, they are a significant source of employment. And yet the productivity and profitability of this local activity pale into insignificance compared with that of the export sector. In the super-market and in any ordinary market there are apples and citrus fruits from the United States. They are better quality and often even cheaper than the Jamaican products. The local farmers are in a cleft stick. The cost of their fuel, seed, fertiliser and equipment is rising, whereas the prices for their produce are falling. And credit at the bank is expensive or impossible to obtain.

For that reason more and more small farmers are resorting to the culti-vation of ganja, the local name for marijuana. For many impoverished farmers it is practically the only way of earning any money. Conditions for the production of ganja are ideal: a tropical climate, fertile soil and a not easily accessible interior. In addition, the most important export market, the United States, is not far away. The farmers plant ganja in small quantities between their other crops. Looking after the plants is a time-consuming job but it is worth the effort. The *sensi* or *sensimilla*, one of the best qualities of ganja, brings in eight to ten thousand Jamaican dollars per kilo. A quarter of an acre can yield one kilo of ganja; if the farmer tends his ganja well, two harvests a year are possible.

Ganja has unofficially become an important export product. Apart from the farmers, small dealers and big dealers earn handsomely from the drug trade. They obtain the dried and baled ganja from the farmers and trans-port it to the dozens of illegal airfields or to the waiting boats on the coast. Sometimes the ganja is even sent conventionally by scheduled air-craft to the customer. On a number of different occasions Air Jamaica has had to pay a heavy fine to retrieve its aircraft in which US drug enforce-ment agents had discovered huge consignments of ganja. In addition to pilots, the police, government officials and even politicians form part of the 'ganja connection'.

With 76,000 tons produced in 1992, Jamaica was far from able to meet that year's permitted EC import quota of 105,000 tons. Without preferential treatment in the European market of both Jamaican sugar and Jamaican bananas, as determined by the Lomé Agreement, these important agricultural sectors would be in a parlous state. As it is, the risk remains that cheaper Latin American bananas may yet force down the price of Jamaican fruit, even with the special protection afforded by the EC.

Other export crops are cocoa, coffee, coconut, pimento and citrus fruits. With the exception of citrus fruits, production is mainly in the hands of small farmers. The cultivation of citrus fruits, such as oranges, grapefruit and ortaniques has undergone considerable expansion in the last twenty years. Medium-sized commercial companies are prominent in this specific area of agriculture.

In contrast to an expanding agricultural export sector, production of food crops for domestic use is flagging. In the 1980s the farmers who grew crops for the Jamaican market lost a lot of ground to cheaper food imports from abroad. The dependence on imported foods is particularly high, with 66 per cent of foodstuffs coming in from abroad. These include such staples as flour, rice, fish and tinned milk. Jamaica, like many other developing countries, is increasingly producing what is does not consume and consuming what it does not produce.

The informal sector   In times of recession the last port of refuge is the so-called informal sector. Directly and indirectly, an estimated 350,000 people are active in this 'free-range' economy. The 'rented dread', as the male prostitute who offers his services in tourist areas is called, is part of it, but so is the market-woman or 'higgler' and the street trader. Earnings in this sector are highly unreliable and on average are well below those in the formal sector. There is also a complete absence of any legal regulations.

Behind the apparent chaos of informal trade there lurks a well-organised network. And organisation is undoubtedly necessary, because it is not always easy to come by goods and hard currency. Because of the debt crisis and repeated devaluations of the Jamaican dollar, the banks strictly limit the availability of American dollars. Nevertheless, for a shopping trip abroad you need at least five to ten thousand dollars.

The traders, mostly women, go abroad to stock up on clothing, shoes, cosmetics and domestic goods. In Curaçao, Panama and Haiti special tax-free zones have been set up for this trade, while Miami and New York are also of interest because of the much lower prices for electronic goods and cosmetics in particular. The higglers usually find accommodation with their counterparts in these countries, meaning that they can save on hotel bills. They are also able to haggle over the prices they pay because they buy in relatively large bulk lots.

Street trading along a road
through the Blue Mountains.
(Jan Stegeman)

Checking in at any of these places for the flight or boat back to Kingston and passing customs control in Jamaica involve constantly recurring rituals of fierce verbal exchanges which normally end up with the handing over of the necessary bribe. Everybody shares in the profits of this lucrative trade: the customs officer, the porter, the taxi driver and even the government, because at the moment it is impossible to obtain foreign currency at the bank and to clear goods without a payment certificate of income tax and social security.

Informal trade, with its low overheads, is cheaper than its formal counterpart. By means of the informal sector, the impoverished population can get hold of most basic necessities at prices significantly lower than those in the supermarkets. Informal trade has become an essential link in the chain of the Jamaican economy, in which there are countless connecting links between the two sectors.

New hotel complexes   The fastest growing sector of Jamaica's economy is at present tourism. After its decline in the 1970s and the beginning of the 1980s a revival followed in the next decade. In recent years, record after record has been broken. In 1992 one and a half million tourists visited the island, attracted by the superb beaches on the north coast and providing Jamaica with an income of US$815 million. Tourism has now become the coun-

Many tourists arrive in the
Caribbean by cruise ship.
(Jan Stegeman)

try's most important source of foreign currency (in 1992 bauxite and
alumina accounted for US$577 million). The private sector is investing in
tourism to the full. In various places along the north coast, new complexes
of hotels and apartments are springing up, while existing ones are being
modernised. Even the government gives a high priority to tourism by
improving services and infrastructure. It is investing, with foreign aid, in
a new road to Negril on the west coast, for example, and Montego Bay
airport is being modernised. New markets are being tapped; after the
Americans, Canadians, British and Germans, the Japanese are the latest to
discover Jamaica's beauty.

Tourism brings in dollars and work for Jamaica. Nevertheless, even this
sector is vulnerable to changes in the economic tide. Since Jamaica is not
the only island in the region to go for tourism, competition and price-
cutting are inevitable. Jamaica has also suffered from some adverse public-
ity concerning attacks on and harassment of tourists, but the authorities
rightly point out that the island is safer that many North American cities.

Industrial exports   Development of the import substitution industry – the strategy
deployed for the first time during the 1960s and pursued up to the 1980s –
has not been entirely productive. Jamaica's domestic market is too small.
The profits obtained from it do not balance the costs of importing raw
materials, fuel, technology and know-how.

Hurricane Gilbert

Every year hurricanes sweep through the Caribbean. On 10 September 1988 satellite photographs warned that a tropical storm was building up some four hundred kilometres south-east of Puerto Rico. It was christened Gilbert, and was the seventh that season.

That same evening Gilbert developed into a full-blooded hurricane, as the tropical cyclones in the Caribbean are called. Every day the atmospheric pressure at its centre decreased. On Monday 12 September the centre of Gilbert passed just below the Dominican Republic and Haiti. Damage was considerable since the area battered by winds at hurricane force and velocity was between 150 and 200 kilometres in diameter. The hurricane then changed course, making straight for Jamaica. And there Gilbert reached its climax. The eye of the storm precisely followed the island's longitudinal axis. Wind velocities of 280 to 300 kilometres per hour left a trail of devastation across the entire island.

Agriculture suffered damage estimated at US$300 million. Entire harvests were lost. Uprooted trees and crop-plants were dragged along in the force of the wind and the water. It was to be three or four years before production of coffee beans, cocoa, sugar-cane and citrus fruit was again at its former level. The production of bananas was still not back to its former level in 1993. Thousands of cattle drowned in the rivers which, as a result of the extremely high rainfall, had swollen to unprecedented levels. Industry and the service industry were also severely affected. For six weeks most businesses were at a standstill and community life was disrupted for months on end. Not until just before Christmas did most districts in the capital, Kingston, have electricity again and in the interior the supply of electricity had not been fully restored one year later. Because of damage to pumps, purification plants, pipes and buildings the supply of drinking water was disrupted over a long period of time and water had to be brought by lorry to the most critically affected areas. Distribution of emergency supplies was seriously hampered by lack of material and infrastructural damage. Telephone and telegraph communications were inoperative for months because of damage to masts, lines and buildings. The destruction of roads, houses, schools and hospitals only served to exacerbate the problems. Ninety per cent of school buildings suffered damage; of the island's 25 hospitals two were completely destroyed and eleven seriously damaged. The devastation was highest in the slum districts. The number of dead was, in view of the damage, relatively low: 45. Hurricanes occur so frequently in Jamaica that the inhabitants are well used to protecting themselves.

Industrial production for export offers more opportunities. This has certainly been the case in light industry such as the textile and clothing sector as well as the food-processing and the drinks industry. More than 100,000 Jamaicans are employed in these businesses, which are mostly located in the industrial zone on the west side of Kingston. Enlarging access to the US market, an integral part of the Caribbean Basin Initiative, was a huge impetus, since now low wages are Jamaica's greatest trump card. Jamaica is currently one of the biggest suppliers of underwear to the US market. The Caribbean Common Market (CARICOM), meanwhile, is even more important for industrial exports. Three-quarters of exported Jamaican industrial products go to CARICOM countries.

In the future Jamaica's industry will have to contend with the North American Free Trade Agreement (NAFTA) between Mexico, Canada and the United States and with competition from Latin American countries. Further economic collaboration at the regional level in the Caribbean will therefore be increasingly a part of Jamaica's industrial strategy.

■ CARICOM: Caribbean integration

With its 2.5 million inhabitants, Jamaica is one of the larger nations in the Caribbean, with far fewer people living on the other English, French and Dutch-speaking islands. From the point of view of industrial potential, Jamaica stands head and shoulders above most other Caribbean countries. Only Cuba, the Dominican Republic and Puerto Rico, the last-mentioned because of its special relationship with the US, are economically more powerful.

Given the islands' small domestic markets and their disproportionate dependence on one or two export products, the need for regional economic collaboration goes without saying. And yet this has always proved difficult to get off the ground, as in 1962 when the West Indies Federation ended in fiasco.

In the 1960s and 1970s most of the British colonies in the Caribbean became politically independent. First Jamaica and Trinidad (1962), then Guyana and Barbados (1966) and later the smaller islands in the eastern part of the region severed their constitutional links with London. In the course of time, the leaders of the new states became convinced of the necessity of a common economic policy. But how far that collaboration should extend has always been a burning issue. As a prominent country, Jamaica plays an important role in the debate on regional collaboration.

At first there was little enthusiasm in Jamaica for collaboration with the other islands. In 1968, for fear of being excluded, the JLP government did, however, join the Caribbean Free Trade Association (CARIFTA). That treaty removed trade restrictions, quotas and tarriffs, meaning that the regional market for the various products was considerably enlarged. Jamaica

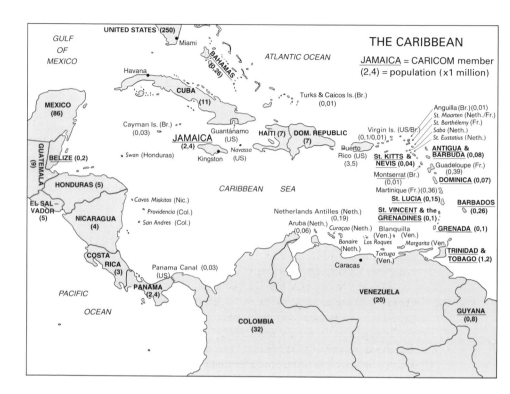

THE CARIBBEAN

JAMAICA = CARICOM member
(2,4) = population (×1 million)

continued systematically to oppose all attempts to bring about further collaboration, even after its exports to other states in the region had increased.
Nor at first did Jamaica want to participate in the Caribbean Development
Bank, as the government feared that it would have to subsidise the
vulnerable small economies of the East Caribbean islands and that it might
lose control over its own financial and economic policy. Consequently,
very little came of the joint agreements – a common external tariff,
harmonisation of investment premium policy and joint development
projects. Only under Michael Manley's government in the 1970s did the
tide turn. Manley gave new impetus to the debate on further integration.
He was convinced that only with a strong regional economic policy could
the otherwise insignificant Caribbean economies make their presence felt
on the world market.

Oil crisis   In 1973 Jamaica became one of the founders of the Caribbean Common
Market (CARICOM). CARICOM wished to bring about further integration by
means of a common market, collaboration in areas such as healthcare,
education, transport and collective formulation of foreign policy. The ink
on the signatures was not even dry when all such worthy objectives were

rudely shattered by the consequences of the oil crisis of 1973-4. Oil-producing Trinidad enjoyed an abundant harvest from the rising oil prices, but the economies of the other islands were dealt severe blows. It also became clear that in times of adversity, the regional spirit was likely to give way to national self-interest.

Jamaica, as did also other CARICOM countries, concluded bilateral oil supply contracts with oil-producing Venezuela and Mexico, much to the displeasure of Trinidad. Protective measures taken by the individual economies did not improve relations. Eventually CARICOM did survive the economic crisis but there was little enthusiasm for further integration. Plans for enlarging the organisation by including countries such as Haiti, Surinam, and the Dutch and the French Antilles were shelved as a result of political differences of opinion.

In the 1980s the Reagan administration's Caribbean Basin Initiative brought about new tensions in CARICOM. While Prime Minister Edward Seaga set himself up as the regional executor of US policies, other government leaders in CARICOM raised objections to the political conditionality of Reagan's CBI (economic aid in exchange for *inter alia* free elections) and they accused Jamaica of profiting most from the CBI.

During recent years the readiness to collaborate at the regional level has increased. In 1991 Prime Minister Manley was the CARICOM chairman, a chance he seized to stimulate further integration. The formation of economic blocs in the world (European integration, NAFTA) is a new impetus for the creation of a more effective Caribbean common market.

During a CARICOM summit in Basseterre, St Kitts, in 1991 government leaders agreed to set up a common market in 1993. The target date was later put back to the year 2000. It has since been agreed that implementation of monetary union and harmonising of fiscal and trade policies will be staged. Yet at the summit of October 1992 supranational issues were again shown to be highly sensitive. The proposal to appoint a CARICOM Commission, a day-to-day executive with more powers (on the lines of the European Commission), was rejected. Instead, there will be a CARICOM Bureau, in which three government leaders of members states will sit.

Enlargement of CARICOM to include other, non-English-speaking countries in the Caribbean, such as Surinam, Puerto Rico, Haiti and the Dominican Republic, will now, it seems, have to wait somewhat longer.

4   SOCIETY

The quest for the promised land

Anybody travelling along the magnificent north coast can scarcely imagine that the majority of Jamaicans live a marginal existence. On this coast there are the chic tourist hotels, the extravagant country houses of rich Jamaicans and the modern housing complexes with weekend cottages for the middle class. Only miles away inland, in small ramshackle villages and rural slum settlements, there are pockets of extreme poverty.

Since independence the distribution of income has become more and more distorted. Poverty is greatest in the rural interior and in the slum districts of the large towns, where living conditions are often appalling. Here, only one in ten dwellings is connected to mains water and the supply of electricity is not much more widely available.

The IMF-approved policy of retrenchment in the 1980s and the enormous increase in the cost of living have distorted income difference even more. Those who do have work have less and less to spare. Ten per cent increases on the price of a bus ticket have not been unusual in recent years, and similar rises have affected fuel oil and rent, as well as basic foodstuffs and many other everyday necessities.

Growing numbers of people without regular work have to rely on the informal economy. Women are particularly vulnerable to the consequences of the economic malaise. The unemployment figures for women are twice as high as for men. In Jamaica there are many one-parent families: in four out of ten families the woman is the sole breadwinner. There is no general unemployment benefit. The very poorest can obtain food coupons (usually fifty Jamaican dollars a week) under the provisions of government poverty alleviation schemes or from the National Insurance Fund. In 1991 some 125,000 Jamaicans were forced to resort to these inadequate state hand-outs. Symptoms of malnutrition have been increasing in recent years. In the leading children's hospital in Kingston the number of children admitted for malnutrition and related diseases has tripled since 1978.

■ Migration

Foreign countries   Since the last century emigration has been a way out of Jamaica's social and economic malaise, and many Jamaicans have left to look for work abroad. Most of them remained there as long as they had a job and then returned to their own country. Others took up permanent residence in countries such as Great Britain, Canada and the United States.

Kingston.
(Jan Stegeman)

The first great migration for work took place in the 1860s, when many Jamaicans left for Panama to help with the first attempt to dig a canal through Central America. The project, under the direction of the French diplomat Ferdinand de Lesseps, failed through incompetence, corruption and an epidemic of yellow fever. A US construction team tried again at the beginning of this century – this time successfully. Most of the labour force employed in the building of the Panama Canal were again Jamaicans, who were badly paid and segregated from the North American workers.

Many Jamaicans also went to work on the banana plantations in Costa Rica and Honduras, and later on in the Cuban sugar and coffee plantations. They were in demand because they worked hard, were paid little and did not tend to agitate for better conditions. Some stayed to live in these countries, married and built their lives there.

The greatest emigration exodus was to the United States, beginning even before the Second World War. Unhindered by the strict immigration conditions which exist today, many families made the crossing and landed up in the great port cities – New York, Baltimore, Boston and Philadelphia – in the north-east. Today, approximately 350,000 people in that region are of Jamaican origin.

After the war the United States restricted immigration, and consequently many Jamaicans went to Canada and Great Britain. Between 1950 and

1960, 200,000 moved to Great Britain to work in such areas as nursing and transport, until there too the immigration laws were tightened. Since then, in fact, some women and children have managed to emigrate to join family members, but the overall rate of migration has dropped drastically. People of Jamaican origin live principally in London, Birmingham, Manchester and Liverpool. While many have succeeded socially and professionally, there are still a disproportionate number of Afro-Caribbean families living in Britain's depressed inner-city areas.

In spite of restrictions on immigration into the rich countries, the number of people emigrating from Jamaica is rising. In 1990 alone, 25,000 people left the island to start a life somewhere else, more than twice the total for the previous year. Every year thousands emigrate illegally to their rich neighbour, the United States. One consequence of emigration is that the population of Jamaica is growing only very slowly compared with that of other developing countries: between 1982 and 1988 by some 1.7 per cent annually. Without emigration, it has been estimated that growth would be 2.3 per cent. Emigration is also economically important, as in many poor villages and slum districts a regular remittance cheque from a relative working abroad is perhaps the only reliable source of income.

The city: Kingston   The small spit of land on which the Norman Manley international airport is situated offers a wonderful view of the Jamaican capital on the other side of the water. Kingston lies locked in between the foothills of the Blue Mountains and the city's natural harbour. The coastline is now dominated by modern high-rise buildings. The old piers, where the ocean-going vessels moored up, where the famous stepped ashore and from which many thousands of Jamaicans left for Canada and Great Britain, have long since made way for a new concrete business centre.

Behind this, the city sprawls out like a huge fan onto the slopes of the mountains. Perhaps midway between sea and mountains, off Half Way Tree, another cluster of high-rise buildings can be seen: New Kingston. This is the latest city extension, with head offices of banks, foreign companies, embassies and modern shopping arcades. Real city life is played out in the main streets of downtown Kingston. The pavements are the domain of the street traders. There is one very popular spot, in particular, under the arcades in the once majestic King Street. The arcades provide shelter against the fierce sun and are the most important pedestrian routes for office workers and business people. This is the preferred sales patch for the 'sky juice' seller with his barrow of ice and cordials, the market woman with piles of fruit and the vendor with cheap razor blades and toothbrushes. This is where the city seethes with life, this is where it becomes clear why hundreds of thousands of Jamaicans prefer life in Kingston to life in the interior. Here there is a chance of earning something.

COLOURS AND PEOPLE

Yellow (gold) symbolises the sunlight and the rich natural resources; black stands for the problems people must overcome. Agriculture and hope for a better future are represented by the colour green.
(Source: Flags Documentation Centre of the Netherlands)

Reggae star Ziggi Marley continues the tradition of his father Bob Marley.

Seaford Town. Shop owner of German descent with his son and neighbourhood children.

Tourist paradise on the northern coast.

Taking zebu cows to pasture beside a field of sugarcane near Port Antonio.

Almost ready for the beach.

Sunday morning, on the way to the church

Colour photographs by Michael Kooren

Hats and bags for sale to tourists.
Ocho Rios.

At the market.

Cricket – the national sport.

School crossing in Kingston.

Downtown and uptown   In the last thirty years Kingston has grown with enormous speed and the old town has been flooded with newcomers, as the population rose from 376,000 in 1960 to more than 700,000 in 1990. Most have gravitated to the west side of the city centre, where traditional neighbourhoods have declined and the slum districts have spread out: Trench Town, Jones Town, Denham Town, and in the east right up to the foot of the Long Mountains communities such as Franklyn Town and Rockfort – a broad swathe of poverty and pauperisation, where street gangs rule the roost. Sometimes there are neighbourhoods, such as Tivoli Gardens, which stand out because of their better housing. These are isolated attempts on the part of politicians to deal with inner-city squalor and to win the support of the community.

The well-off and even the middle classes rarely venture into the old city. They live their life 'uptown' in suburbs such as Cherry Gardens, Arcadia Gardens, Constant Spring and Forest Hills. These names evoke a completely different life. Here, the rich have impressive villas with magnificent gardens, tennis courts and swimming pools. Those who live here do their shopping in modern shopping centres, which resemble those of any North American suburb. The latest status symbol is the satellite dish which brings the world of US consumerism directly into the sitting-room. This luxury is protected by fences, guards and dogs. Not surprisingly, private security is currently one of Jamaica's fastest growing industries.

■ Social services

Healthcare   *'Paying off our foreign debt has become more important than the lives of the poor'*, wrote Archbishop Samuel E. Carter in his pastoral letter of 1991.

Poverty-related diseases such as typhus and cholera, which had for a long time been under control in Jamaica, are now beginning to surface again. A whole variety of symptoms connected with malnutrition are also on the increase. What is most alarming is the structural deterioration and budgetary decline of healthcare. In the mid-1970s about nine per cent of the government's budget went on health; in following years expenditure was cut back to an average of five per cent.

Jamaica's healthcare system was once considered good. The British left behind them a network of hospitals and health centres, both in the towns as well as in the rural villages. With more than twenty hospitals and some 350 health centres, the spread of provision across the island is still quite adequate. But the picture is less favourable if we look at the staffing and the equipment of these medical facilities. In 1971 there was approximately one doctor for every 2,600 of the population, but there is now still only one doctor for every 2,040. From 1975 on, the number of hospital beds has been cut back and there is a serious shortage of nursing staff. Jobs in healthcare have simply become unattractive because of low salaries and poor working conditions, and many qualified doctors and nurses choose to go abroad to make their career. Since 1990 the government has been pursuing an active promotion policy to interest people again in the medical profession. One recent measure was a doubling(!) of salaries.

Because of privatisation measures and cuts in the public sector, healthcare costs have risen sharply. The Jamaican Planning Office has calculated that four people in ten among lower-income groups are forced to make use of private medical care. The prices of medicines have also risen to exorbitant levels in recent years, and most poorer people are no longer able to buy even necessary medicines. Semi-privatised and under-funded, healthcare in Jamaica has become a luxury commodity.

Education Up to the mid-1970s Jamaica had no grounds to be ashamed of the level of its education provision. Education was almost entirely in state hands and a great deal was being invested. That era has passed as a result of the debt crisis, and during the 1980s education has been systematically dismantled. Annual government spending per student fell from US$120 in 1980 to US$97 in 1987. By way of comparison, Barbados spends US$600 a year for every student, while in Trinidad and Tobago the figure is US$550. In 1975 almost eighteen per cent of the government budget was still being spent on education; by 1985 this had dwindled to eleven per cent.

The results of this policy can be seen daily: overfull classrooms, decaying buildings and outdated or inadequate teaching materials. Old school buildings are not being properly maintained and there is scarcely any new building. Many primary and secondary schools do not even have adequate supplies of drinking water or appropriate sanitary facilities. Because of poor working conditions and low salaries, a considerable proportion of teachers and lecturers have turned their backs on education, while those who have stayed are forced to supplement their earnings in the informal sector. In order to be able to meet necessary costs, including salaries, schools have to resort to fund-raising activities such as 'fancy fairs', shows and festivals. Fixed financial contributions are required of the parents.

This is in itself a problem for poor Jamaicans. The number of children attending primary school has fallen by seven per cent in recent years while during the same period the actual number of children of primary school age has increased. These figures are even more alarming given the fact that the majority of poor children only attend primary school. Surveys show that sixty per cent do not complete their primary education and high costs are frequently given as a significant reason. These figures do not say anything about the quality of education, but other surveys reveal that of the children who do complete their primary school education more than half are 'functionally' illiterate.

The situation in secondary education is not much better. Both the level of attendance and the level of achievement are below standard in comparison with other English-speaking Caribbean countries. For instance, in 1975, 7,000 students took the GCE 'O' Level English examination and sixty per cent passed while in 1989 only a third passed of the 5,700 students who entered. In the English-speaking Caribbean, only the results in Guyana and Grenada are worse, yet in 1981 Jamaica was still among the three top countries with the best education results.

■ Violence

'Five dead in city shootout', 'Elderly couple murdered: twelve murders so far this week', 'Gang warfare breaks out', 'Wave of violence sweeps over Jamaica'. These are a few recent headlines.

Once again a wave of violence is sweeping across this Caribbean island. And once again there is general indignation. Violence in Jamaica is the talk of the day. Since the 1970s the country has had to deal with an astronomical increase in the number of crimes of violence. In the period between 1974 and 1990 the number of cases of reported rape, mugging and robbery doubled. In the same period the number of deaths due to violence increased even more sharply. In the 1980s the number of people who lost their lives each year as the result of criminal acts was around five hundred. In 1990 there was a noticeable increase: that year alone, 700 Jamaicans died violent deaths. The election year 1980 brought a depressing peak, as during the election campaign between 1,200 and 1,300 Jamaicans lost their lives in political turmoil.

Street gangs   Life in the towns and, above all, in Kingston is particularly violent. In the slum districts boys get into ganglife all too quickly, drawn by the identity and protection the gang or 'posse' offers and which family and school are often unable to provide. Stealing brings in food, money and a sort of street credibility. Often the boys are still teenagers when they are sucked into the spiral of violence. In the beginning they stand guard while the older gang members do the job, but they learn quickly how to use a revolver or a rifle. After a period of apprenticeship, they join in the muggings or robberies themselves. Much gang activity is connected to the drug trade, and some gang members, known popularly as 'yardies', are active in international drug trafficking.

Shootouts between street gangs and the police are an everyday event. There are places in Kingston which are off limits to the police and where the gangs are in charge. Police are regularly victims of assault, attacks and reprisals. In return, at the police station and in prison, the police are all too ready to take their revenge with frequently brutal mistreatment of suspects and prisoners.

The heavily-guarded Gun Court prison in Kingston.
(Marcel Bayer)

Police violence Legislation to deal with violence has been tightened up in the last thirty years. In the mid-1970s the Manley government set up what was called the 'Gun Court'. This area of land in Kingston, surrounded by barbed wire and tall lookout towers, has become a symbol of the way in which Jamaican society has been infected by violence. In the Gun Court summary justice is meted out and the armed gangs are given heavy sentences. With such draconian measures, the police and the judiciary are better able to act, but the excesses of the police in the execution of their duties have likewise increased. Human rights organisations in and outside Jamaica have regularly produced reports of unwarranted police brutality in arrests and in prisons over recent years. The absurdly high number of 'murders' by the police is striking: 206 in 1980, 319 in 1981, 216 in 1985. Compared with, for example, the United States these figures are extreme (in New York in 1985 there were twelve deaths caused by police). In no other democratic western country has police brutality resulted in so many victims.

The Americas Watch Committee concluded in 1986 following an investigation that the police were even carrying out summary executions. Low morale in the police force and frustrations over low salaries and lamentable working conditions were, according to the human rights' commission, the principal causes of police violence. In the last few years police violence, at least as regards fatalities, has receded. Nevertheless, 145 of the 700 reported deaths due to violence in 1990 were attributable to police action.

In May of that year, for example, three prisoners were killed during a prison revolt in St Catherine. Hospital staff later revealed that the bodies of the prisoners showed signs of serious maltreatment. Police violence continues, in spite of the sharper concern for the issue in Jamaica itself and in spite of the heavy sentences which have sometimes been meted out to the guilty police officers.

Another area of human rights concern is the unusually large number of convicted criminals who are awaiting execution on Jamaica's 'death row'. Estimated at 270, some of these men have waited for up to fourteen years for their sentences to be carried out.

In 1993 the unsuccessful 'Operation Ardent' was replaced by the Anti-Crime Investigative Detachment (ACID), special combined police and army units which operate in the large towns and tourist areas. ACID has been criticised for its alleged brutality and for its unfortunate acronym, which seems to disregard the fact that many attacks in the ghettos of Kingston involve burning with acid. Again, the government has opted for the tough approach, despite the failure of similar tactics in the 1970s and 1980s.

■ Religion

Sundays in the Jamaican countryside, and the same scene always unfolds: small groups of adults and children walk along the roads in the hills and villages, all dressed in their best clothes and some holding a bible. After the long journey from isolated farms and settlements, they meet in the little parish churches which can be found in every village, however small, in the island. A little later, the sound of prayers and hymns, accompanied by guitar and tambourine, is carried on the warm tropical breeze.

Many younger people in the towns are turning away from the church with its 'vain hopes and empty promises'. But rural people, especially the elderly, are still deeply religious, seeing their faith as a source of comfort and hope. The most important church communities are the Anglicans, the Baptists and the Church of God, but there are also Methodists, Roman Catholics, Mormons and, of course, the Rastafarians. In addition, Jews, Hindus and Chinese also have their own religious services.

For a long time the slaves and the planters each had their own religion until the growth of the Baptist and Methodist churches in the 18th century. The spiritual nature of these new churches won over many slaves to the faith, particularly since these non-conformist churches were more openly sympathetic to the position of the black population and their interpretation of the Bible was broader than that of the white masters. From these congregations emerged charismatic leaders, Samuel Sharpe and Paul Bogle, who led the people in the political and social struggle.

Rastafarians The Rastafarian movement is a classic example of a religion which has evolved out of resistance to existing society. The movement harks back to old African traditions and is based on its appeal to black consciousness.

Rastafarian and his daughter.
(Maya Pejic)

Ecstasy

In the colonial period everything possible was done to outlaw African heritage and belief systems. But African influences have survived; in the *kumina*, for example, a mixture of the West African words *akom* (being possessed) and *ana* (ancestors). *Kumina* is very similar to *voodoo* and *winti* in other countries, and plays an important role at birth, puberty, marriage, sickness and death. The ritual is accompanied by a great deal of dancing and ecstatic music, rum and ganja. In the ecstasy the spirits of deceased ancestors reveal themselves to those who become possessed. Sometimes they tell of calamities, sickness and curses; sometimes they warn of impending danger.

In 1930 the Rastas appeared for the first time in the streets of Kingston: a handful of 'dreads', named after the strange way they wore their hair. The movement swiftly became a synonym for rebellion against existing norms, its members causing a sensation, not just because of their appearance, but also because of their remarks about the white race, the superiority of the black race and their wish to return to Africa as soon as possible. The coronation of the great grandson of King Saheka Selassie of Shoa as Emperor Haile Selassie of Ethiopia on 2 November 1930 was the long-expected portent of this return. The new Emperor, who, as they were convinced, was descended from the great Ethiopian kings of the Old Testament, was the Messiah and the Supreme Authority of the uprooted black population in the world. He would bring them back to the Promised Land.

The Rastafarians – the name refers to Selassie's aristocratic title – immediately fell out with the authorities, and confrontation and conflict surrounded the movement's early period. The Rastas were accused of undermining authority and of subversive practices, and were regularly sentenced for illegal possession and use of ganja (marijuana).

Since then, the movement has grown to become an accepted folk culture. The number of active Rastas in Jamaica has been estimated at more than 100,000, but the number of sympathisers is much greater. Their cultural influence is undeniable. Reggae, to a large extent based on Rastafarian ideology and imagery, has become a long-lived international musical trend. The Rastafarian movement's influence can also be found in other forms of cultural expression such as painting, poetry and dance.

Biblical customs The appeal to religion is central to Rasta beliefs, and the Bible is the starting-point for faith and daily life. Most Rastas know what are for them important Bible passages by heart. *'Better is a dinner of herbs where love is, than a stalled ox and hatred therewith'* (Proverbs 15.17) is guidance as regards their diet, while *'They shall not make baldness upon their head, neither shall they shave off the corner of their beard...' (Leviticus* 21.5) is the theological basis of their distinctive hairstyle.

Rastas are convinced of the inevitable destruction of Babylon, which for them is synonymous with white western culture, as has been proclaimed in the Day of Judgement. In opposition to corrupt, decadent and immoral white civilisation, the Rastas advocate a way of life which is in harmony with the Old Testament. They reject the staples of western consumption, such as coffee, meat or alcohol, but ganja is an approved 'holy herb'. This they see as a source of wisdom and insight, as can be read in Psalm 104.14: *'He causeth the grass to grow for the cattle, and herb for the service of man.'*

Deep religious feelings and the emphasis placed upon the Bible are part of the Rasta conviction that biblical tradition does not belong to whites

The Marcus Garvey statue stands
in front of the Public Library in
St Ann's Bay.
(Jan Stegeman)

Marcus Garvey and black consciousness

A Jamaican who made an important contribution to the self-awareness of
the island's black population was Marcus Garvey, whose fame also reached
far beyond the borders of the Caribbean island.

Garvey was born in 1887 in St Ann's Bay on the north coast of Jamaica.
At a very early stage in his life he had become familiar with the poverty
and deprivation experienced by the black working class and peasantry in
Central America, the Caribbean and the United States. In the US he set up
the Universal Negro Improvement Association with the goal of improving
the position of black people throughout the world. The organisation aimed
eventually to set up its own independent black state in Africa. For this
purpose, Garvey created the Black Star Steamship Line, and in order to
promote the black cause he published his own magazine, the *Negro World*.
Marcus Garvey's strength lay in the fiery rhetoric with which he awakened
black pride. He told his audiences that it was high time to finish with end-
less slavery and discrimination. '*Stand up, you mighty race, you shall achieve
whatever you want*' was one of Garvey's stock phrases.

But his 'inflammatory' speeches made Garvey unpopular with the whites
and inevitably with the US authorities. In 1919 he survived a serious
physical assault, and in 1925 he was accused of fraud in connection with his
shipping line. He was deported.

■

Back in Jamaica, Garvey tried to resume his work but he had little success. In the elections of 1930 he and his followers could only win one seat on the colonial Executive Council. Convinced that he was being obstructed in his work, he again decided to leave Jamaica. He continued his campaigning in London, where he died in 1940 of a heart attack. Not until 1964, after independence, were Garvey's services to Jamaica recognised. His remains were flown back to Jamaica and he was proclaimed a national hero.

alone. In fact, even more radically, they reject the 'white' interpretation of the Bible, which they see as a religious arm of colonialism. Rastafarianism teaches that for centuries black people have been indoctrinated with the idea that that they had no cultural and religious traditions. Africa was a 'dark' continent, without civilisation. The image of God and Christ, they believe, has been coloured by such prejudice in order to justify slavery.

The Rastas idealise Africa, which is synonymous with Ethiopia and which stands for a rich and powerful culture. They also adhere strongly to the ideas of black leaders such as Marcus Garvey who spoke of African 'redemption' and the eventual return of all Africans to their Promised Land.

Yet, most Rastas today no longer aspire to being repatriated to the land of their origin. The death of Haile Selassie, the ensuing civil war and the famine in Ethiopia are certainly contributory factors. More generally, Rasta organisations have begun increasingly to concern themselves with Jamaican society and particularly with the position of the poor and the black community.

The influence of the Rastas goes further than the obviously recognisable 'dreadlocks'. With their symbolism and trenchant indictment of existing society, they are a powerful and compelling presence among the militant younger generation of the ghettoes. But Rastas are more than a protest movement or a subculture. Many prominent people in artistic and scientific circles, in the media and even politicians have been influenced by their philosophy. Among black Jamaicans the movement has strengthened feelings of positive identity and self-esteem, even if many people still consider the Rastas as socially undesirable.

The Rasta is proud of his own individual identity, something which is expressed in the language he speaks, with its emphasis on the first person. *We* has become *I and I*. *I* emphasises individuality, independence and originality, as distinct from *me,* the form of the first person singular which has become standardised in Jamaica. This is why the *I* is to be found in many words which have become metamorphosed in Rasta idiom: *I-rie* is 'good' or 'positive', *I-tal* means 'natural' or 'vital', 'divine' becomes *I-vine*, and 'brother' becomes *I-bro*.

5   CULTURE

The cradle of reggae music

It is Friday evening, Rockfort's night out. In a bare hall, which normally does duty as a neighbourhood centre, heavy bass is booming out of the loudspeakers. Under a minimum of lighting people are dancing and smoking. On entering, the visitor is greeted by the aroma of ganja.

Behind the sound system, of which the only visible thing is a panel full of flickering light-bulbs, the disc jockey mixes the music with special effects to create a rhythmic whole. The disc jockey, also called rapper or toaster, talks over the music with his own words in patois, the Jamaican dialect.

The 'sound system dance' is the disco of the working-class suburbs. Here the people make their own music based on the reggae rhythm. Long before rapping got to the United States and Europe the disc jockeys in Jamaica were inventing their own lyrics in this way. In the rich people's discos of New Kingston, one can hear the latest hits from America and England.

■ Reggae, rappers and DJs

Disc jockeys have always played an important part in Jamaica in the spreading of new musical styles. In the 1940s they travelled through the villages and the sugar plantations with their mobile discotheques. Between the records they filled in with fast-moving introductions and improvisations. At the same time, they would also bring important news to people. According to some, this custom harks back to the 'talking drum' tradition of West Africa, where stories are told to an accompaniment of rhythmic drumming.

Through the development of technology in the record industry and especially the success of reggae, the disc jockeys in Jamaica could develop a style of their own. You can see it in every slum district among the toasters or rappers who organise a weekly disco evening. They are street poets, social commentators, they derive their lyrics from everyday life. A life without prospects perhaps, but hope, the erotic and religion are also popular sources of inspiration: *'A thing that existed from Adam and Eve went up my sleeve and never came down till Christmas Eve'*.

Winston Foster, better known as Yellowman, an albino, is the most popular of the rappers. At every big music festival, King Yellowman is the absolute top of the bill. He has been banned several times on the radio for

Three DJs in a ghetto

'Music is a way of forgetting misery. If you've got nothing to do then somewhere there's always a session going on, a poor man's disco. For us DJs it's a way of escaping the ghetto.' Mr Chin, Harron Man and Mr German are three young disc jockeys from Waltham Park, a slum district in West Kingston. They are waiting in one of the rooms of Tuff Gong International, the studio set up by Bob Marley and now run by his wife. Displayed on the wall are numerous photographs of famous reggae stars; most, of course, of Bob Marley himself. Since the Tuff Gong Studios moved to West Kingston, the three DJs can be regularly seen in the vicinity, just like many other young Jamaicans. They hope at some time to be able to make a record. *'Only with the backing of an organisation can you get anywhere. Foreigners come to Jamaica to see the artists who have spread the reggae message all over the world, but we ourselves can't afford the admission tickets to the concerts. Now we want to profit from the fame as well'*, Mr Chin explains.

Mr Chin, Harron Man and Mr German are the toasters in their own district. They have their own equipment, two decks, an amplifier with a mixer panel and four enormous speakers which they built themselves. Their lyrics relate to everyday life. *'We don't need to wait that long for inspiration'*, says Mr Chin. *'The situation in the ghetto is worse than ever. Most of the younger people have no work. The "politricks" of the government have made life impossible for ordinary Jamaicans. Music is the way out for the youth of the ghetto, the alternative to violence and crime.'* Mr German adds: *'Yellowman and many other artists come from the ghetto. Reggae still means "comin' from the people".'*

The three DJs from Waltham Park have now put their best numbers on a tape and are hoping that one of the studios in Kingston will see something in it. But competition is fierce. As Mr German says: *'Everyone wants something for themselves. If you are successful that provokes aggression in the others. Everybody wants a share, a "piece of the meal". Fights and jealousy are the downside of success.'*

his smutty lyrics but the disco regulars love them for their 'slackness' or explicit erotic content. 'DJs have taken over reggae' was a recent headline in the *Daily Gleaner*, Jamaica's most important newspaper. Yellowman is the uncrowned king of the rappers.

Bob Marley   *'He's a king, he's a legend [...] he put together nations and people'*. In the national stadium in Kingston homage is being paid to Bob Marley. The whole of his family is there, together with many musicians who worked with the king of reggae. The audience sways and joins in, humming to the

During a concert in 1976,
Bob Marley got political rivals
Michael Manley (left) and
Edward Seaga (right) to join in
a symbolic handshake.
(Adrian Boot/Camera Press)

sound of Marley's famous songs. For a moment it seems as if time has
stood still. Then Ziggi Marley, the eldest son, leaps around the stage in
the characteristic manner of his father, as if attempting to breathe new life
into the Marley legend. *'Jah Rastafari'* he roars into the microphone. The
audience reacts with wild enthusiasm. *'This is reality you know...Rise all
falling fighters. Rise and take the stand again. Rise and start your fight
again'*.

Some thirty years have passed now since four boys from Trench Town,
one of the slum districts in downtown Kingston, set up their first serious
band: Junior Braithwaite, Peter (Tosh) Macintosh, Bunny (Wailer)
Livingston and Robert Nesta Marley. They called themselves the Wailing
Rude Boys, later shortened to the Wailers. They interpreted the feelings
and ideas of young people of the ghetto. It was the period of the Rude
Boys, militant youngsters in the slum districts who were protesting against
the discrimination and oppression felt by the black majority in Jamaica. It
was the period of riots, looting and shoot-outs.

The music of the Wailers consisted of a combination of various musical
styles, such as rhythm and blues, elaborating on the rhythms of ska and
mento (Jamaican folk music). In its early stages the music was banned by
the authorities because it was supposed to be subversive and inflammatory.
For that reason reggae music was not at first played on Jamaican radio,
where imported American and English music set the tone.

Nashville in Kingston   Much has changed and the music of the ghetto youth of Jamaica has
conquered the world. Reggae has become a major force in international
music. Every country, from the United States to Japan, has got its reggae

bands. Jamaica itself, and above all Kingston, has become for reggae what Nashville has become for country and western music. It now has its own record industry and there are internationally famous studios which specialise in recording reggae. International reggae stars like Peter Tosh, Jimmy Cliff, Burning Spear, Bunny Wailer, Yellowman and Third World began their careers in these studios. Above all, it was Bob Marley who spread the style of music and the message over the whole world. Marley gave reggae a more commercial flavour by adding a rock rhythm, perhaps at the expense of originality but nonetheless increasing its accessibility. The adulation of Marley reached almost religious proportions. His funeral on 21 May 1981 (he died of a brain tumour) was like that of a head of state. Since then a statue has been erected to him, right next to the national stadium in the Park of Fame. In his characteristic pose, wearing jeans and denim shirt, the left hand on the neck of his guitar and the right hanging loosely on the strings, he has been given a place among the other national heroes of Jamaica.

Reggae is still alive and well. Many young people see in the music industry a chance to escape their hopeless situation in the poor districts. But the competition, as well as the jealousy, is considerable and only a few are destined to have a real career in music.

■ Cricket, the national sport

Jamaica is known in the West for its athletes and particularly its sprinters, of whom the most famous and controversial is Ben Johnson. Jamaican women athletes have built an enviable reputations in short distance track events.

Yet the real national sport on the island, just as in the other former British colonies in the region, is cricket. The game was introduced to the Caribbean by the English in the colonial period but only since the 1930s has cricket been fully cultivated by the black inhabitants of the islands – with great success. For decades the joint West Indian team has been playing world-class cricket. Cricket has perhaps done more than anything else to cement a sense of regional cooperation between the English-speaking islands – and to emphasise their difference from those which play baseball.

The high point of the season is the encounter between the two best teams in the world. In this contest the West Indies regularly prove themselves superior to countries such as Australia, New Zealand, India, Pakistan and South Africa. Nevertheless, the greatest triumph is always the occasion when victory is scored over the former English motherland.

During international matches between the Caribbean states, national feelings run high, particularly when the Jamaican team plays Trinidad or Barbados. Sabina Park, the Kingston cricket ground, is filled to capacity on such occasions and throughout the entire island fans sit glued to the tele-

vision. Jamaica has produced celebrated cricketers, often men from poorer
districts who became the idols of their generation as a result of their skills.
George Alphonso Headley was one such idol. His father came from Barbados but he grew up with his mother in Jamaica. In the 1930s he created a
sensation in Jamaican and West Indian cricket and for many Headley is the
best batsman that the region has ever produced. He is certainly in any list
of the all-time world best.

One match which he played in London against the favourite of the day,
England, has become a legend. Even the partisan English spectators gave
him an ovation for his two centuries in one match. His double century in
such a highly-charged game and on the 'holy' cricket ground at Lord's is
even today regarded as unique.

The fame of Headley and other outstanding cricketers has been an enormous asset for the sport's development. Cricket at club level has grown
strongly over the last few decades and new talents regularly come to light,
succeeding in getting into the West Indian team and achieving international fame. This naturally encourages younger people to go in for the
game, as top-class cricket offers status and prosperity. Even in the remotest
corners of the island there is always a small field or a yard somewhere
where boys with their makeshift wickets and bats practice their skills as
batsmen, bowlers or wicket-keepers.

■ Festivals

It is hardly surprising that the Jamaican people with their varied ethnic
origins and mix of cultural influences, should have produced so many
artistic talents. Cultural life is rich and varied. Many Jamaicans see their
country as the cultural heartland of the English-speaking Caribbean.

The high point of the cultural season comes in summer. While carnival
time is being celebrated on other islands in the Caribbean, Jamaica is
dominated by Reggae Sunsplash and the Festival. During Sunsplash in
Montego Bay reggae lovers from all over the world gather for three days to
listen to old and new stars. And all the big names come too. For at Sunsplash old friends meet, new talent is discovered, business is done and
drink and ganja are never in short supply.

The apotheosis of the cultural year is the Festival, held in the weeks
leading up to Independence Day on 6 August. Plays are performed at
various venues, there are music and dance shows and visual artists exhibit
their work. The centre of activities is Kingston, where amateur artists who
have come through the earlier rounds meet each other in the finals. Schools
are particularly active in this cultural competition.

Source of inspiration   With its spectacular tropical landscapes, Jamaica has always
attracted artists from all over the world. Since the 1940s famous writers,

singers and film actors have paid visits to the island to enjoy its idyllic nature. Some, such as Noel Coward, Ian Fleming and Errol Flynn, took up residence here for shorter or longer periods of time and some used the island as an inspiration for new work.

The Jamaican artists who made a name for themselves earlier this century were very strongly influenced by art trends in the United States and Great Britain. An exceptional artist such as John Dunkley (1881-1949), a barber from Kingston, who had a style of his own, was hardly understood and was dismissed as an eccentric. His 'primitive' representations, often with bizarre details and proportions, were widely rejected as 'un-European'. Yet, today Dunkley's pictures are priceless. After independence in 1962 there was a general revival of the original themes and traditions of the mixed population, often with great artistic virtuosity. In almost all forms of Jamaican art there are elements which echo African and Asiatic rituals and which relate to life in the countryside or in the city.

By means of a progressive art policy, particularly from the 1970s onwards, moves are being made to stimulate the interest of young people with an aptitude for different forms of art. In 1976, for instance, the Cultural Training Centre was set up which offers training courses in painting, music, dance and acting. In less than twenty years it has become a seed-bed of talent.

Dance and theatre Few islands the size of Jamaica can boast an internationally recognised 'in-house' dance institute. The National Dance Theatre Company of Jamaica, or NDTC for short, has this reputation and has enraptured audiences not just in the region, but far beyond in all parts of the world.

The NDTC has its home base in the Little Theatre in Kingston. The ensemble consists of dancers, singers and musicians and it puts on performances which are based on Jamaican history and daily life. On one occasion life in the ghetto may form the central theme; on another, the dancers may draw on African rituals or on Rasta culture. The play *Court of Jah*, for example, is entirely devoted to the music of Bob Marley. The choreographies are grafted upon a mixture of indigenous, classical and modern influences.

The leading figure behind the NDTC is Professor Rex Nettleford, who from its very beginning in 1962 has guided the dance theatre as its director and choreographer. Nettleford is intensely interested in everything to do with the identity of black Jamaicans and is the author of many books on the subject, including the highly influential *Mirror Mirror* (1970). Nettleford's passion for exploring African themes and art forms can be clearly seen in the work of the NDTC.

The Ward Theatre in Kingston is
the mecca of Jamaican pantomime.
(Jan Stegeman)

Pantomime   Jamaican pantomime is genuine folk theatre. Pantomime is a lively and
irreverent musical production with lyrics in patois, the Jamaican dialect.
Performances are full of allusions to social life and politics, and the
characters are caricatures of well-known figures in Jamaican society. The
origin of the pantomime goes back to the time of the Jamaican Little
Theatre Movement, the oldest theatre company in the Caribbean. This
company originally put on classical fairy tales such as Sleeping Beauty
and Cinderella, but later on more characters were used from local folk
culture as a starting point, as, for example, Anansi the cunning black
spider and hero of countless Caribbean fables.

   The Ward Theatre in old Kingston is the pantomime mecca, and the
season falls in the first few months of the year when the latest work is put
on. For designers of costumes and scenery, composers and directors it is
effectively the highest honour to be allowed to collaborate in this national
pantomime production. Audiences come from the whole of Jamaica, young
and old, rich and poor, to the 'Ward' to gape, to chuckle, to laugh and to
swing along with the spectacle.

CONCLUSION

Little Jamaica possesses great riches. Since the colonial period, however, most of its riches have been disappearing abroad. The economy depends almost entirely on demand for Jamaican products in the markets of rich countries, whether those products be bauxite and aluminium, ganja or tourism. This dependence is not likely to go away in the near future simply because the domestic market is too small to sustain a non export-oriented development model. Jamaica is not the only country with an open and dependent economy; the entire Caribbean suffers from the same weaknesses. This much was recognised even before the independence. Even in the 1950s and 1960s there were compelling arguments for regional collaboration. In the event, the idea of unity and collective action was killed off because those of nationalism and self-interest were stronger.

The time is now ripe for collaboration. One by one, the Caribbean islands have over the last few decades been forced to face their own limitations. Jamaica, too, has become sadder and wiser. From outside, a world increasingly made up of trade blocs is forcing the Caribbean countries to rebuild links and jointly to map out the future. Without collaboration, for example in the expansion of CARICOM, they will never be able to escape the vulnerability of being 'micro-states' in a region of powerful blocs and alliances. Besides, experience has proved that it is unwise to stake too much on support, in whatever form, from Washington. In a post-Cold War era, the Caribbean is no longer a foreign policy priority for any US administration, and aid and investment have fallen dramatically. In the first instance, the Caribbean will have to look after its own interests.

Jamaica has picked up the threads of the integration process which in 1962 had been left lying loose. The island can do this with some pride for, as opposed to other young states in the region, democracy in Jamaica has weathered all the storms. It is true, of course, that the quality of Jamaican democracy can be faulted in many ways and violence and corruption remain widespread. But Jamaica has not experienced coups or dictatorship and has always enjoyed freedom of the press and an independent judiciary.

Intensive collaboration with the other states in the vicinity (and not only the English-speaking ones) can further stabilise that democracy. Ultimately, with joint forces, a real attempt can be made to build a solid economic base in all those countries which are now afflicted by dependence, instability and chronic social inequality.

FURTHER READING AND ADDRESSES

Americas Watch, *Human Rights in Jamaica.* New York, 1986.

Barrett, L.E., *The Rastafarians, the Dreadlocks of Jamaica.* Kingston, 1977.

Beckford, G. and Witter M., *Small Garden, Bitter Weed: Struggle and Change in Jamaica.* London, 1980.

Black, C.V., *History of Jamaica.* London, 1983.

Blume, H., *The Caribbean Islands.* London, 1976.

Cordingly D. and Falconer, J., *Pirates: Fact and Fiction.* London, 1992.

Girvan, N., *Foreign Capital and Economic Underdevelopment in Jamaica.* Kingston, 1972.

Insight Guides, *Jamaica.* Kingston, 1990.

Kirton, C., *Jamaica: Debt and Poverty.* London, 1992.

Levitt, K.P., *The Origins and Consequences of Jamaica's Debt Crisis, 1970-1990.* Kingston, 1991.

Manley, M., *Struggle in the Periphery.* London, 1982.

Nettleford, R.M., *Mirror, Mirror: Identity, Race and Protest in Jamaica.* Kingston, 1970.

Owens, J., *Dread, the Rastafarians of Jamaica.* Kingston, 1976.

Payne, A.J., *Politics in Jamaica.* London, 1988.

Social Action Center, *Hooked on Debt.* Kingston, 1990.

Stone, C., *Democracy and Clientilism in Jamaica.* New Jersey, 1980.

Stone, C., *On Jamaican Politics, Economics and Society: Columns from the Gleaner.* Kingston, 1989.

Thomas, C.Y., *The Poor and the Powerless: Economic Policy and Change in the Caribbean.* London, 1988.

Trade and Travel Publications, *The Caribbean Islands Handbook 1993.* Bath, 1993.

Williams, E., *From Columbus to Castro: The History of the Caribbean.* London, 1970.

Wilson, M., *The Caribbean Environment.* Oxford, 1989.

Witter, M. and Kirton, C., *The Informal Economy in Jamaica: Some Empirical Exercises.* Kingston, 1990.

FICTION

Patterson, O., *The Children of Sisyphus.* London, 1983.

Senior, O., *Summer Lightning.* London, 1986.

ADDRESSES

Jamaica Tourist Board,
1/2 Prince Consort Road,
London SW7 2BZ
Tel. 071-224-0505

Jamaica Tourist Board,
866 Second Avenue
(2 Dag Hammarskjold Plaza),
New York, NY 10017
Tel. 212-688-7650

Transatlantic Wings/The Caribbean Experience,
70 Pembroke Road,
London W8 6NX
Tel. 071-602-4021

British High Commission,
26 Trafalgar Road,
Kingston 5
Tel. (809) 926-9050

US Embassy,
Mutual Life Centre,
2 Oxford Road,
Kingston 5
Tel. (809) 929-4850

FACTS AND FIGURES

See also reference map

A   GEOGRAPHY

Official name: Jamaica.
Situation: Jamaica lies in the Caribbean Sea, between 17°43-18°32N and 76°11-78°21W, it is one of the Greater Antilles; the island is 240 km in length and 80 km at its widest.
Surface area: 10,991 km².
Administrative division: 14 parishes; the parishes of Kingston and St Andrew together form the Kingston Metropolitan Area. The division into three counties (Cornwall, Middlesex and Surrey) is now hardly ever used.
Capital: Kingston, over 700,000 inhabitants (1991).
Other towns: Spanish Town (100,000 inhabitants), Montego Bay (75,000).
Infrastructure: relatively well-developed road network: 16,638 km (1984) mostly asphalted; most important roads are the ring road around the island and the cross-land connection Spanish Town-Ocho Rios; rail network: 339 km, for passenger traffic the line from Montego Bay to Kingston is particularly important; international airports: Kingston and Montego Bay; principal port: Kingston.
Relief and landscape: Jamaica is mountainous and more than half its surface lies more than 500m above sea level; on the eastern side of the island the landscape is dominated by the Blue Mountains, the highest point being

Time difference
London 12.00 noon
Kingston 7.00 a.m.

Blue Mountains Peak (2,292m); the Rio Grande, with many rapids and waterfalls, is the longest river; the middle and west of the island consist of limestone plateaus, which have taken on strange shapes under the influence of wind and weather; in particular, Cockpit Country in the north-west is littered with river basins, *poljes, mogotes,* cockpits, steep river valleys and caves; on the northern and western coasts there are magnificent beaches.
Temperature and rainfall: Jamaica has a tropical climate (savanna climate); the winds from the north-east ensure a fair amount of rain on the north side of the mountains (2,500-5,000mm per year); there is much less precipitation on the south side of the mountains (on average 1,250mm); the differences in height and precipitation bring

about very sharply differing average temperatures: at the coast temperatures can rise to 32°C/90°F (July), in the Blue Mountains they can fall to 6°C/43°F (January); most of the rain falls in May and June and in September and October; the coolest period is November-April.
Earthquakes and hurricanes: Jamaica is situated in an area where hurricanes occur regularly; the last great hurricane, the most severe ever to strike Jamaica, was Gilbert in 1988; Jamaica also lies in an earthquake zone as the Caribbean is a geological area where various plates press against each other; Port Royal was devastated in 1692, Kingston in 1907.
Flora and fauna: although the original vegetation has disappeared, the Jamaican plant-world is one of fascinating richness and beauty; some 3,000

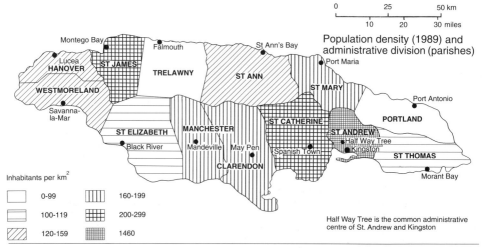

JAMAICA

0	25	50 km
10	20	30 miles

Population density (1989) and administrative division (parishes)

Inhabitants per km²

☐ 0-99	▥ 160-199
☐ 100-119	▦ 200-299
▨ 120-159	▦ 1460

Half Way Tree is the common administrative centre of St. Andrew and Kingston

flowering plants occur, many hundreds of which cannot be found anywhere else in the world; there are, for instance, 200 varieties of orchid, 60 varieties of bromelia and hundreds of varieties of fern; among the indigenous plants are guava, breadfruit and star apple; inseparable from the exotic world of plants and flowers is the doctor bird, a songbird with a brightly-striped tail; many varieties of parrot, parakeet and finch populate the forests; crocodiles are still to be found in the interior, as are other kinds of reptiles.

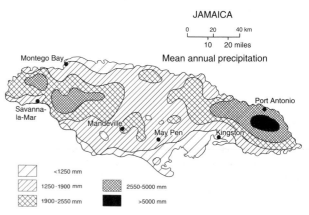

JAMAICA

0	20	40 km
10	20 miles	

Mean annual precipitation

▨ <1250 mm	
▨ 1250-1900 mm	▦ 2550-5000 mm
▨ 1900-2550 mm	■ >5000 mm

B

POPULATION

Population (1991): 2.5 million; national census 1982: 2.2 million.
Population growth 1980-1990: 1.3%; 1990: 0.9%.
Population density (1990): 216 inhabitants per km².
Urbanisation (1990): 52%; beginning of 1970s: 44%.

Age structure (1990): 0-14: 34%, 15-64: 59%, 65+: 7%.
Birthrate (1990): 24.3 per 1,000; in 1975: 30.3; in 1965: 38.2.
Mortality rate (1990): 6.5 per 1,000; in 1975: 7.7; in 1965: 8.7.
Infant mortality (1990): 16 per 1,000 children under one year of

age.
Average life expectancy (1990): 73 years; in 1975: 69, in 1965: 65.
Doctors (1988): 1 doctor per 2,040 inhabitants; 1 per 1,993 in 1965; 1 hospital bed per 370 inhabitants (1986).

Per capita calorie consumption (1989): 2,609.

Adult illiteracy (1990): less than 5%.

Education (1989): 100% of children attend primary school and 61% continue studying; there is 1 teacher for every 32 children in primary school, 1 for 57 in 1965.

University: University of the West Indies at Mona, Kingston, with many students from other English-speaking Caribbean countries; in addition, a number of higher vocational courses; many Jamaicans study in the US, Canada and Great Britain.

Social Development Index (UNDP Human Development Index 1993): 69th, high position in middle group, (UK 10th, US 6th position) total 173 positions.

Age-sex pyramids of Jamaica (1985) and the United Kingdom (1989)

Ethnic composition: blacks and mulattos 91%, whites 4%, Indians 3.5%, Chinese 1,5%.

Language: English, also patois, English interspersed with many African words.

Religion: Protestants 23%, Baptists 18%, Anglicans 15%, Roman Catholics 8%, Methodists 6%, Presbyterians 5%, Church of God etc.

C

HISTORY AND POLITICS

Some key dates: • circa 700 BC: the Arawaks settle on Jamaica • 1494: Columbus 'discovers' Jamaica and lands in Dry Harbour, now Discovery Bay, on 4 May • 1509: Juan de Esquivel is the first Spanish Governor • 1517: the first African slaves arrive in Jamaica • 1534: Spanish Town (Villa de la Vega) founded as the capital • 1640: sugar introduced as a trading crop • 1655: English expedition led by General Venables and Admiral Penn, the Spaniards surrender (11 May) • 1670: Peace of Madrid (8 July), Jamaica becomes British • 1692: Port Royal, the pirate capital, destroyed by earthquake • 1738-9: First Peace Treaty with the Maroons • 1795-96: Second Maroon War • 1805: slave trade banned in British colonies

• 28.12.1831: great slave uprising in St James under the leadership of Sam Sharpe • 1834: abolition of slavery becomes official; in disguised form slavery lasts a further four years in Jamaica • 11.10.1865: Morant Bay Rebellion • 1866: Jamaica becomes a crown colony • 1872: Kingston becomes the new capital • 1907: earthquake destroys large part of Kingston • 1938: fierce social upheaval and riots, political parties and trade unions are formed • 1944: new constitution, the first general election is won by the Jamaica Labour Party (JLP) of Alexander Bustamante • 1955: the opposition party, the People's National Party (PNP) wins the elections, Norman Washington Manley becomes prime minister • 1957: full

internal self-rule • 1958: Parliament of the West Indies Federation (WIF) set up in Port of Spain, Trinidad • 1961: following a referendum, Jamaica withdraws from the WIF • 1962: full independence (6 August), JLP government • 1972: Michael Manley's PLP wins the elections • 1976: another victory for the PNP • 1980: break with the IMF, JLP wins elections, Edward Seaga becomes prime minister • 1982: President Reagan visits Jamaica • October 1983: Jamaica supports US and Caribbean intervention in Grenada • 1984: early elections boycotted by PNP, one-party parliament • 1988: Hurricane Gilbert causes great destruction • 1989: PNP wins the elections, Manley again prime minister • 1992: Prime Minister Manley resigns for health

reasons, Party Chairman P.J. Patterson becomes prime minister • 1993: Prime Minister Patterson wins convincing election victory over Edward Seaga.
Constitution: Jamaica is a constitutional monarchy within the British Commonwealth.
Head of State: Queen Elizabeth, represented by a governor-general nominated by the prime minister; the government is elected on a constituency voting system; the parliament consists of two chambers: the House of Representatives has 60 members elected by majority vote in the 14 parishes, the Senate has 21 seats, 13 of which are appointed by the prime minister and the remainder by the governor on the basis of nominations by the leader of the opposition.
Political parties: People's National Party (PNP), Jamaica Labour Party (JLP), Workers' Party of Jamaica (WPJ).
Armed forces (1989): land forces 2,500, coastal defence 200, airforce 150.
Membership of international organisations: UN and UN organisations, British Commonwealth, Caribbean Common Market (CARICOM), Organisation of American States (OAS), Latin-American Economic System (SELA), Lomé Agreement (ACP country, associated with EC), Movement of Non-aligned Countries.
Media/communications: 67 telephone connections per 1,000 inhabitants (1986), 149 TV sets per 1,000 inhabitants (1986); the largest (morning) newspaper is the *Daily Gleaner;* the same company publishes a smaller-circulation evening newspaper, *The Star;* other morning papers: *The Herald, The Observer;* television and radio are provided by the Jamaica Broadcasting Corporation (JBC), which is owned by the state; there are also private radio stations.

D

ECONOMY

Currency unit: Jamaica dollar; J$ = US$: 8 (1990), 21.5 (1991), 22.2 (1993).
Gross National Product (GNP): US$3.5 billion (1991).
Per capita GNP (1991): US$1,475.
Economic growth: 1980-1990: 1.6% per year, 1991: 0.2%.
Foreign debt (1991): US$4.5 billion.
Debt servicing as % of export earnings and services (1990): 31%.
Development aid (1990): US$280 million, 7% of GNP, US$82 per capita.
Structure of the economy (1965/1990): percentage of GDP by sector: agriculture 10/5%, mining 20/26%, industry 17/20%, service industries 53/49%; working population by sector (1965/1989-91): agriculture 37/25%, industry 20/12%, service industries 43/63%.
Unemployment: 30%; informal sector: 35%.
Private cars per 1,000 inhabitants (1987): 19; UK 333, US 588.
Exports (1990): US$1.4 billion; main products: bauxite and alumina 60%, sugar 11%, clothing 5%, alcoholic beverages 3%, fruit 3%.
Imports (1990): US$1.7 billion; main products: oil, foodstuffs, machinery, chemical products.
Principal trading partners: exports: US, Venezuela, United Kingdom, Canada, CARICOM; imports: US, United Kingdom, Canada.
Tourism earnings (1991): US$870 million.

E

JAMAICA AND BRITAIN/UNITED STATES

Trade relations with Britain: Jamaican exports to Britain in 1992 totalled £127 million; principal export goods were sugar (£44 million), fruit (£41 million) and bauxite (£26 million). British exports to Jamaica in 1992 totalled £43.5 million; principal export goods were industrial machinery (£15 million), other manufactures (£11 million) and chemicals and fertilisers (£5 million).
Trade relations with the US: Jamaican exports to the US in 1992 totalled US$599 million; principal export goods were bauxite, sugar and fruit and vegetables. US exports to Jamaica in 1992 totalled US$938.5 million; principal export goods

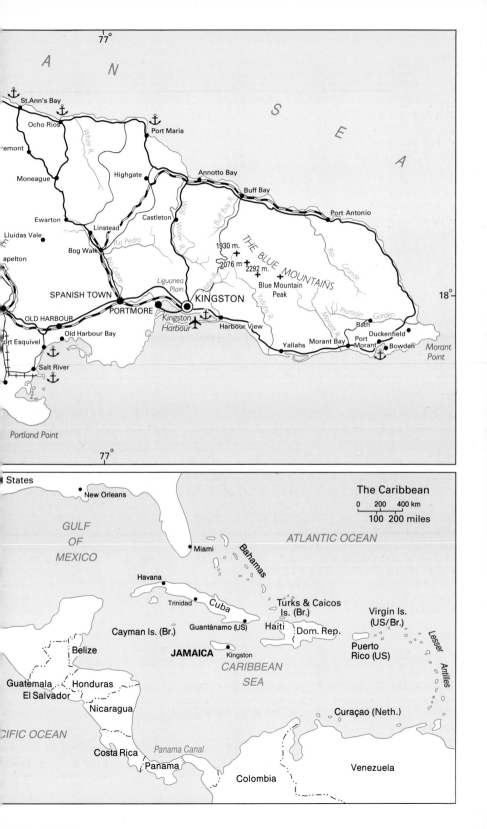

Top map (Jamaica)

77°

A   N

S

E

A

St. Ann's Bay
Ocho Rios
⚓
remont
Moneague
Highgate
White R.
Port Maria
⚓
Annotto Bay
Buff Bay
Port Antonio
Ewarton
Linstead
Castleton
Lluidas Vale
Bog Walk
apelton
Rio Pedro
Rio Cobre
Wag Water R.
Buff Bay R.
Rio Grande
THE BLUE MOUNTAINS
1930 m. ✝
2076 m ✝
✝ 2292 m.
✝ Blue Mountain Peak
SPANISH TOWN
Liguanea Plain
PORTMORE
KINGSTON
18°
OLD HARBOUR
ort Esquivel
Old Harbour Bay
Kingston Harbour
✈
⚓
Harbour View
Yallahs R.
Morant R.
Plantain   Garden
Bath
Duckenfield
Salt River
⚓
Yallahs
Morant Bay
Port Morant
⚓
Bowden
Morant Point

Portland Point

77°

Bottom map (The Caribbean)

States

The Caribbean

0   200   400 km
100   200 miles

New Orleans

GULF
OF
MEXICO

Miami

ATLANTIC OCEAN

Bahamas

Havana
Trinidad
Cuba
Cayman Is. (Br.)
Guantánamo (US)
Turks & Caicos Is. (Br.)
Haiti
Dom. Rep.
Virgin Is. (US/Br.)
Belize
JAMAICA
Kingston
Puerto Rico (US)
Guatemala   Honduras
El Salvador
Nicaragua
CARIBBEAN
SEA
Lesser Antilles
Curaçao (Neth.)
CIFIC OCEAN
Costa Rica
Panama Canal
Panama
Colombia
Venezuela

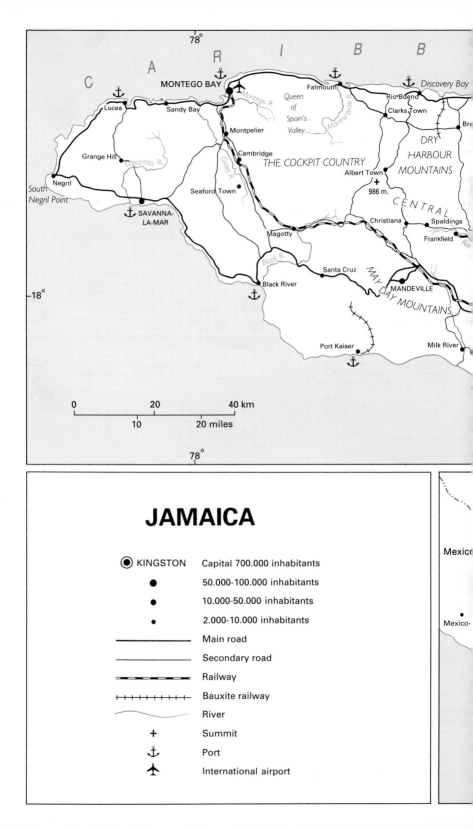

ere oil, machinery, chemicals,
lectrical goods and foodstuffs.
*id and development relations
ith Britain:* in 1991/2, official
British bilateral aid to Jamaica
was £4.2 million. The principal
British development agencies
uch as Oxfam, Christian Aid
nd CAFOD all have programmes

in Jamaica, mostly working with
specific target groups such as
small farmers and unemployed
youth.
*Aid and development relations
with the US:* projected official US
bilateral aid to Jamaica for 1994
is set at US$20.2 million; in
1993 the budget was set at

US$66 million. This contrasts
with the US$200 million granted
by the Reagan administration in
1981/2. A wide range of US
agencies and church groups have
development programmes in
Jamaica.

SOURCES

World Bank, *World Development
Report 1992;* Europa Publica-
tions, *South America, Central
America and the Caribbean*

1993; UNDP, *Human Develop-
ment Report 1993;* Instituto del
Tercer Mundo, *Third World
Guide 1991/1992; Latin America*

Monitor, London; Jamaica
Information Service, London.